Visual Project
MANAGEMENT

*The Manufacturer's Guide to
Implementing the Theory of Constraints*

*Projects in Less Time:
A Synopsis of Critical Chain*

Visual Project
MANAGEMENT

▷ ▷ ▷ ▷ ▷ ▷ ▷ ▷ ▷

Simplifying Project Execution
to Deliver On Time and On Budget

MARK J. WOEPPEL

For more information contact:
mwoeppel@pinnacle-strategies.com
65050 W. Park Suite 306-335
Plano, TX 75093

ISBN paperback: 978-0-692-42325-7
ISBN eBook: 978-0-692-42326-4

Library of Congress Control Number: 2015938015

CONTENTS

Acknowledgments

Rarely is something completely original invented; we all "stand on the shoulders of giants" in the creative process. The work of Sanjeev Gupta of Realization Technologies and Eliyahu Goldratt was foundational to the approach we created. Thank you.

There were also several people who slogged through early versions of the manuscript and provided insight and correction, and, in some cases, stories that were used in the book. To my colleagues at Pinnacle Strategies: Orval "Duke" Porritt, Cory TerEick, Trevor Calder, Stephane Luthi, and Ian Wong, thank you for your contribution to this work. It would not be what it is without your help.

Last, and probably not least important, are my clients, many of whom have become personal friends.

Thank you for entrusting me with your business; I learn something new on every project—and some of it is actually useful! My wish is that you see yourselves in these pages in a flattering light.

The fact that many projects are delivered late and over budget is widely known, but rarely acknowledged. The frequency with which they fail is astonishing. Whether the project is to implement a new technology strategy, or a capital project, they require significant investments that last months or years. For organizations that commission these projects, the underwhelming track record of delivery combined with the investments creates significant risk.

To reduce this risk, many organizations have invested in their project management capabilities. Yet, despite spending millions of dollars in training and the development of greater project management maturity, the ability to consistently execute on time and on budget eludes us.

If you're an executive that commissions these projects, you should be well aware of these risks. It should be no surprise if an established company fails in the coming years because of an out-of-control project, because the data suggests that one or more will.[1]

We at Pinnacle Strategies reached this depressing conclusion in 2014 after commissioning an independent study[2] of project management practices and results from around the world. We examined the survey responses from over 4,000 project managers and senior executives, comparing their budgets and estimated performance benefits with the actual costs and results. Their projects ran the gamut, from large IT projects to engineering, procurement, and construction (EPC) projects, to strategic business initiatives. Most were expensive—for large IT projects, the average cost was $167 million, and the largest was $33 billion—and many took several years. Our sample drew from respondents around the world, but we found little difference among them in the results.

We found that project cost overruns were commonplace. For example, a recent Accenture survey[3] found

---

1 (Flyvbjerg, September, 2011) Why Your IT Project Might Be Riskier Than You Think
2 (Pinnacle Strategies, 2014) Training and PMOs Will Not Save Our Projects; The State of Project Management Practice and Effectiveness.
3 Accenture, "Developing Strategies for the Effective Delivery of Capital Projects," 2012.

that more than 30 percent of capital projects are now completed over budget, and more than 35 percent of projects are finished late.

The problem isn't that we don't have enough skills, training, or centers of excellence. It's that what we do have is focused on control: scope, change, stakeholder management, etc. We have very little ability to consistently execute projects on time or on budget in the face of a constantly shifting reality.

Clearly something is missing from project management practice. What are the principles and best practices for delivering projects on time and on budget? Should we accept the "generally accepted" solution as being the best or correct solution? Should we continue to depend on the "art" of the project manager?

In this book, I'm going to show you the foundational causes of on-time, on-budget project execution. Surprisingly, they have little to do with planning. I, along with my colleagues at Pinnacle Strategies, have discovered that by focusing on the processes and behaviors associated with project execution, executives can govern their portfolios more effectively to deliver projects in less time and at a lower cost. At the same time, the project teams' decision-making processes can be made sharper and better aligned with the entire organization to execute projects when they are most needed, and with less drama.

This book will highlight the core principles that project teams can employ—no matter what environment they're in—to reduce project durations, improve delivery performance, and stay on budget.

I'll be introducing the project execution methodology called ViewPoint. With ViewPoint, you can transform any project.

ViewPoint:

• Eliminates the silo effect on project teams, streamlining and improving communication and accountability;

• Is a streamlined approach to managing project execution, delivering fast, significant results to improve schedule and budget performance;

• Is easily understood, with few obstacles to implementation;

• Can easily be adapted by any organization, regardless of current practice and maturity;

• Works with and complements existing methodologies and software;

- Generates maximum buy-in to changes, or at least generates no significant opposition; and

- Makes completing your projects a satisfying experience, not a battle to win.

If you're a fan of the Critical Chain Project Management methodology, as I am, you'll find a clear path to building your implementation, graduating from simple tactics to sophisticated methods of managing your portfolio with this method. Along the way, you'll be able to engage your teams and your organization with a logical, successful model.

After reading this, you may accuse me of oversimplifying the task of managing projects. I fully understand that not everything that's important can be fully explained in a book of this length. There are plenty of texts about risk management, controls, scheduling, stakeholder engagement, etc. What I hope to do is shed some light on an area of project management that has been overlooked.

Don't forget what managing projects is about—it's not about things, and it's not about procedures or controls. Project management—*successful* project management—is about people.

Portfolio results are generated at the project level, and project results are generated at the deliverables, and deliverables are created by people—your most critical resource—accomplishing tasks. Thus, no portfolio or project manager can improve their results without paying attention to what creates those results. In a sense, your portfolio and project strategy is dependent upon the tactics, and the tactics can dictate the strategy.

With the ViewPoint methodology, you'll find all of the above—in short, successful project management. Throughout this book, I'll explore the philosophy behind effective project delivery, and I'll give you a map that you can use to make it happen in your own organization. I'm going to show you methods, principles, and practices that have worked in multiple environments—consistently. In ViewPoint, you'll find the answer to consistently executing projects on time on budget.

▷ ▷ ▷ ▷ ▷ ▷ ▷ ▷ ▷

PART I

Why Are Projects Always Late and Over Budget?

CHAPTER 1

Unhappy Customers and Blown Budgets

Why Are the Projects I'm Managing
So Freaking Unmanageable?

I made a mistake. No news there—everyone makes them, right? Except this time, it seemed like it was the same mistake I made last time. And the time before that. Our project management transformation pilot project was successful—32 percent reduction in delivery time, and we had happy team members—but nothing was done after that. No expansion. No lasting organizational change. Our team went home thinking, *Shit. What did we do wrong? We can't blame the customer this time.*

I mean, yes, we did have some unexpected organizational challenges. People with no skin in the game were throwing rocks at our team, but that's normal, right? Everyone has an opinion, and they're not shy about sharing it. But the project was successful! That should have silenced the critics. It didn't.

My firm, Pinnacle Strategies, does a lot of project management process transformation work. We implement Critical Chain Project Management, Probabilistic Planning, PMOs, and the like—all focused on delivering projects in less time, on time. This success/failure stung. Eager to figure out what had gone wrong (*again*), I did some soul searching.

This was a large, multinational, market-leading company with a matrixed management team. They had a big problem to solve (from my perspective), but little appetite for large-scale change. There was a lot of value to unlock, but there was no real crisis. So I had several criteria I felt that any solution had to meet. The solution had to:

- Deliver fast, significant results in project performance;

- Be simple, with few obstacles to implementation;

- Be adaptable enough to be implemented easily by any organization , regardless of current practice and maturity;

- Work with and complement existing methodologies and software; and

- Generate maximum buy-in to the changes, or at least generate no opposition.

A pretty tall order. So I put this on the back burner, turning my attention to other urgent matters, like our current projects.

Meanwhile, we were working in Norway, a new market for us, delivering all kinds of quick results and value for our customers using our Rapid Analysis Bottleneck Improvement Teams (RABIT). RABIT is the name of a service that we offer to de-bottleneck a process. It's like a kaizen event, but it typically lasts about ninety days. RABIT uses the theory of constraints to focus the deployment of Performance Management, Lean, and Six Sigma tools, which results in a quick boost in output and productivity.

We were applying RABIT to knowledge work and production processes. We were getting a lot of work, and our customers were happy. The process was delivering big results very quickly. One of the key features of the RABIT is that it uses the Lean practice of visual management. But that's not project management, is it?

Shortly afterward, our firm received a request to

work with a Fortune 100 customer to improve their engineering project output. We couldn't do a full-blown PMO there—they had over 400 projects and 450 engineers, and we only had six months to prove our value. We needed something quick. So we adapted the principles from the RABIT process to manage this portfolio.

It was a spectacular success. The users loved it. There was widespread adoption of this new process and enthusiasm for it (including approval from senior managers). Best of all, there were significant improvements, including a **25 percent increase in productivity in less than six months.**

I got pretty excited. It worked! I thought about my backburner project, my criteria for the solution, and this seemed to meet all of them. But *why* did it work? I wanted our team to be able to do it again for other firms. So we began the journey to understand the principles that had created those results. For four years or so, we worked them out, tested them, and taught them. We tried them over and over—with spectacular results.

So, as a colleague, I want to share with you a project management transformation process that:

- Delivers fast, significant results;
- Has few obstacles to implementation;

- Adapts easily to different organizational cultures;

- Complements existing practices; and

- Generates maximum buy-in to changes.

If you're a project manager or portfolio executive, chances are that you're all too familiar with the panic that sets in as the deadline looms. It seems that right before the project or an important milestone is due to be delivered, the budget is already blown, and yet the team is barely halfway to finishing. At the last heroic minute, you finally pull together a deliverable that satisfies the basic requirements, but it doesn't really make anyone happy—not your team, not your customers, and certainly not you.

You're not alone. Executives, project managers, and portfolio managers everywhere can't figure out why, despite their best efforts, projects rarely meet their schedules and go way over budget. In a recent study, researchers found that most large-scale IT projects have an average budget overrun of 27 percent. What's worse—one in six had an average cost overrun of 200 percent, and a schedule overrun of almost 70 percent.[4]

---

4 Flyvbjerg, "Why Your IT Project Might Be Riskier Than You Think," Harvard Business Review, September 2011.

We can't seem get to the root of it. It happens time and time again. It's not that you didn't create an extensive plan before the project. It's not that you haven't undergone hours and hours of training to learn how to successfully manage projects. It's not that your team doesn't want to get the work done. You're providing what, by all accounts, should be a suitable project structure, providing all the support you can, and supplying state-of-the-art methodologies and training—but you're not getting the payoff.

So what's going wrong?

We can put a name to the problem: **project execution**. My firm's independent research[5] into project performance shows that, despite the fact that we have invested heavily in project management processes and capabilities, delivery and budget performance haven't improved much. In fact, we've found there is an *inverse* relationship[6] between the amount of project management training and actual schedule and budget performance. We are getting better at control, but not better at delivery or budget performance.

Delivery and budget performance are tightly linked (as if you didn't know). If you can meet delivery

---

5 Pinnacle Strategies, "Training and PMOs Will Not Save Our Projects; The State of Project Management Practice and Effectiveness," 2014.
6 PriceWaterhouseCoopers, "Insights and Trends: Current Portfolio, Programme, and Project Management Practices," 2012.

schedules, the budget problem nearly solves itself. So rather than focus on what you spend, I invite you to look at what you *do*. That's where you'll make the difference.

There are five key indicators that typically assess project performance: scope, quality, business benefits, budget, and schedule. Project management skills training results in improvement in three of those factors—scope, quality, and business benefits. But when it comes to budget and schedule, not only is there no improvement, but there's a surprising *decline* in performance when more than 75 percent of project staff have been trained:[7]

Training Impact on Project Performance

Figure 1

Without a doubt, the kinds of training that are currently available are important to any project's success. The Project Management Body of Knowledge (PMBOK®) Guide focuses on achieving more discipline

---

7 PriceWaterhouseCoopers, "Insights and Trends: Current Portfolio, Programme, and Project Management Practices," 2012.

in stakeholders' analysis, planning, scope, quality, risk management, communications, monitoring, and control. It's natural, then, that improving skills in these areas would lead to improvements in those factors. But the unintended consequence of such improvements is a reduction in performance in the areas of budget and schedule—and our projects remain unmanageable. Projects are *so* unmanageable, in fact, that many executives don't believe *any* project can be delivered on time and on budget, so they insist on building healthy contingencies into the project in order to compensate.

I believe the reason for this situation is that project execution, unfortunately, is barely addressed in the PMBOK®. The PMBOK® guide devotes less than 5 percent of its content to execution, the business of actually running a project. When execution *is* mentioned, the guide simply suggests having qualified project managers and an information system. In essence, the planning bit of the project is clearly articulated, so any "qualified" project manager should be able to deliver on that plan.

Clearly, executing projects successfully is nowhere near a science; it's still an art. Planning, estimating, and control are very important to project success, but project teams need more guidance in execution to improve schedule and budget performance.

Successful Project Execution
Boosts Financial Returns

The value to be unlocked by improving execution performance is significant. The financial performance of the "best executors" is well above average—a striking 65 percent better.[8]

Benefits of High Performing Execution

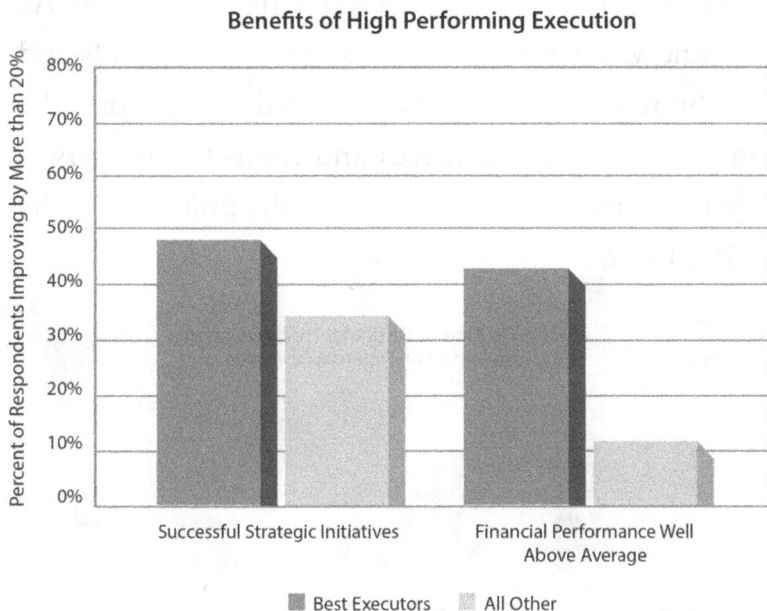

Focusing on just improving on-time and on-budget performance leverages your efforts and results in

8 Lyno Advisors, Inc., Profitable Projects: Transforming Project-Based Operations, 2014.

more financial gain than any other project improvement initiative you could undertake. Companies that improved *either* metric were far more likely to improve on *every* financial metric: Research shows the results of the two respective types of initiatives improving on-time or on-budget performance more than 10 percent versus improving any other aspect of project performance (displayed in figure 2 below). As we know, a big part of the budget equation is found in the management of the schedule. Therefore, the implication for executives and project managers is clear: Focus on the schedule, and the financial results will follow.

**>10% On-Time or On-Budget Improvement
Positive Impact on Financial Performance**

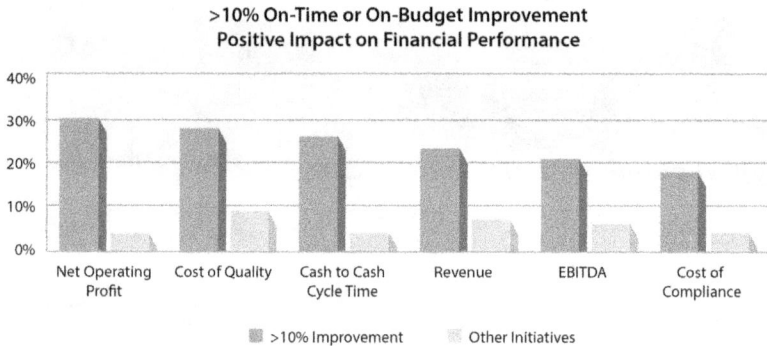

■ >10% Improvement   Other Initiatives

Figure 2

The Core Issues Behind
Late Deliveries and Blown Budgets

There are three primary drivers of performance during project execution:

Situational Visibility – The team can't see and agree on where they are or where they're going.

Management of Variation – the team does not distinguish between the different types of process variation and cannot respond correctly.

Capacity Management – the team cannot adequately plan for or respond to resource capacity shortages.

Situational Visibility: Addressing the Core Problem

An executive who managed a portfolio of projects worth well over $2 billion once said to me, "I do not know where we are, or if we are in trouble or not." Inadvertently, she'd hit the nail on the head and identified the first major problem in project execution: lack of **visibility**. Portfolio managers are turning so many different wheels with so many different cogs that it's difficult to truly see into the projects.

By "see[ing] into projects" I mean knowing, with certainty, how much risk is present in each project, and what specific actions should be taken to reduce that risk. This problem is often attributed to communication. Executives and project managers around the world— nine out of ten, in fact—agree that poor communication is a major contributor to project failure.[9] But what does "poor communication" really mean?

When the individual project contributors lift their heads from their work and trade their individual cubicles for the conference room, is their collaboration a constructive part of the process—or a discouraging exercise in placing blame? Are they able to collectively identify and agree on the priorities of the project? If asked, can they say with confidence, "*This* is the most important thing we should be working on to advance the project"? In organizations with ad hoc project execution processes, there's little transparency: Few people know how their work fits into the whole, or how the project is being addressed in its entirety, so its' difficult to have a conversation about the big picture – the overall project or portfolio.

The team members do not know what really needs to happen in order for them to achieve the end goal. Their individual obligations to the project may make sense to them, but there's no way for them to know how

---

9 Forbes Insights, "Strategic Initiatives Study, Adapting Corporate Strategy to the Changing Economy," 2014.

what they're working on specifically contributes to the grand plan—or how their participation ties in with that of any of the other team members. They can't see what the project's goal is, and you, as the project or portfolio manager, can't support them correctly to ensure that they're helping you to get there.

There is a distinct silo effect[10] in many project teams—the left hand doesn't know what the right hand is doing. Since the people on your team are in the silos, they can't see where they or anyone else are heading. This is one reason our projects are late and end up costing more than we anticipate, and it's also how the quality of the work begins to suffer.

The result is that problems, and their implications for on-time, on-budget deliveries, are identified very late. Communication is delayed. The right problem solvers are brought in too late to prevent the problems, and solving them requires *additional* work. Resource capacity is misused, and the projects are delayed. Costs go up.

This creates a lot of task churning, or as I'll refer to it, multitasking. People frequently stop work halfway through one task to work on another, and they are often

10 The term "functional silo syndrome" was coined in 1988 by Phil S. Ensor, who worked in organizational development and employee relations for Goodyear Tire and Rubber Company, Eaton Corporation, and as a consultant.

pulled from one project and redirected to another. There is a lot of time lost waiting for information, which delays task completion. Priorities shift constantly. Regardless of the reason for the task switching, it means that Project A remains incomplete while resources are diverted to Project B, and we go back and forth between the two. We've set ourselves up to shortchange both projects.

Superior execution demands *informed* collaboration, in which individuals and teams can see beyond the limits of their own tasks to grasp the overall direction of the project. There can be no disagreement about the status of the project. The roles and accountabilities of each team member must be clear. They must focus on what needs to be done *now*, rather than dissecting what has (or has not) been done in the past.

People want to work together, but there is no simple method for them to do so (unless you count your project meetings and e-mail communications as "simple").

Dealing with Uncertainty and Variation: Murphy Lives!

The next key issue is that managers simply don't have the ability to identify (and then compensate for) **uncertainty**. Murphy's law? If it can go wrong, it *will* go wrong. The truth is, projects are full of unpredictability and uncertainty, no matter what we do to anticipate and prevent problems. Uncertainty is probably the single most defining element of projects. There is a lot we don't know—about scope, about work content, about duration, about the weather! Still, we must finish on time and on budget.

Uncertainty exists in projects because variation is elemental to the very nature of things. Projects aren't delivered in spreadsheets or in project management software programs. They're delivered in the real world, where things are kind of messy. You may have created a "perfect" plan that should, in theory, lead you and your team to your goal, but in practice, it can't fully account for *everything* that will actually happen. So you have to find a way to deal with the mess with an imperfect view into the future.

Variation manifests itself as unanticipated events—"surprises"—that derail workflows and delay completions. Crises or emergencies appear out of nowhere. When the unthinkable happens, a snowball effect begins. Tasks can't be completed on time, which rolls into subsequent work streams, ultimately delaying the entire project.

Delay also has a negative impact on the team. We

become frustrated with our inability to make progress, scope and/or budget are sacrificed, and the work product doesn't meet our standards. Everything seems like a fight, and the project suffers. Customers are unhappy, the team is unhappy, and you're unhappy, too. Few people would say, "Working on projects is a wonderful experience!"

You Can't Ignore Resource Capacity

It seems like the number one complaint of project managers is that they don't have enough resources—and they often don't realize it until they're out. This leads to the third and final major cause of failed projects: the inability to integrate information about the **capacity** of resources into project planning and execution decisions. The result is a lack of consideration of information on the quantity and timing of financial resources, subcontractors, *and* the team members.

To get the best results, project and portfolio managers must have an accurate understanding of resource availability, visibility into current and future workloads for those resources, and an ability to make informed decisions based not only on anticipated project loads, but also on the changing needs of the entire organization.

The effect of this lack of information is that project teams simply cannot get the resources they need at the time that they need them. This forces unplanned, last-minute spending to keep the project on track—or it simply delays the project until the resources become available.

Portfolio managers (and leaders of large projects) will prioritize the work across all of the projects, then deploy or redeploy resources based on what is most important for the success of the entire portfolio. A strategic move might be to pull resources off one project to support another project that is lagging. A manager might even decide to allow one project to be delivered late if overall portfolio performance is improved. The portfolio manager needs to be able to assess the impact of different decisions and run "what-if" analyses on different scenarios.

Even if resources are carefully planned and booked in advance, events quickly make this planning obsolete. Most project plans are completed, then stored on a hard drive somewhere or in the cloud, where they become stale and unusable. What's needed is to link the plan and the execution throughout the life of the project, constantly updating the plan as new information becomes available. This consistent updating allows necessary rechecking of resource availability with the plan; it also facilitates the resolution of conflicts.

I can say with confidence that the reason most projects fall short lies not in planning, but in the execution process. For most project teams, the process is simply broken. It's broken in the three aforementioned areas:

- **Visibility:** During execution, the team doesn't know where they are relative to where they need to go—they're in a silo.

- **Uncertainty:** We don't manage variation and uncertainty well.

- **Capacity:** We are unable to integrate information about the availability of resources into project planning and project execution.

I'm going to show you how to systematically address these areas and, as a result, improve your execution process. I'll introduce an execution maturity framework, and as you mature your processes and abilities, your budget and schedule performance will improve as well.

There are twelve principles that translate into practices and techniques for you to utilize while you address these issues, and they're covered in this book. The principles are straightforward, easy to adopt, and will help you improve on your current and future projects. My experience and that of our firm is that when you apply these principles, you will increase the speed of task completions, improve your team's productivity, and boost morale. You'll be able to meet those deadlines and rest within a comfortable budget while doing so.

In the chapters to come, I am going to show you the thinking behind the project planning and execution framework called ViewPoint. I will teach you how to rise to each specific challenge, and help your team achieve that final goal of winning the game—every time. With your win, you'll find happy stockholders, happy customers, happy team members, and a much happier you.

CHAPTER 2

Are You a Project Manager or a Project Micromanager?

Planning—Too Much!

All over the world, promising projects quickly morph into unmanageable creatures, exceeding budgets and eating up time. In response, the collective finger of blame points to everyone's favorite excuse: bad planning. Almost a third of organizations looking to reach higher project management maturity levels say that they have unsuitable succession or contingency plans in place for key project resources,[11] and the most commonly proposed solution to improve project performance is to create better plans.

If bad planning is responsible for failure, then it would of course stand to reason that *good* planning

---

11 PriceWaterhouseCoopers, "Insights and Trends: Current Portfolio, Programme, and Project Management Practices," 2012.

should be the savior. So many of us are conditioned to believe that "a failure to plan is a plan to fail," and we grow confident that successful planning leads to successful project completion.

The old adage isn't necessarily untrue. Having a plan is crucial. But time after time, research has shown that the current and common approaches to planning in project management fail to produce the outcomes that managers expect—and that customers want. Good planning, as it turns out, isn't necessarily the answer; it's part of the problem. This is not because planning in itself is bad, but by focusing on the planning aspect of the project, we aren't looking at the rest of the equation for success.

Peter Drucker said, "…the word 'controls' is not the plural of the word 'control.'"[12] Making a detailed plan doesn't give real control; it gives the illusion of control. What provides control is having an understanding of the interdependencies of the work and having the flexibility to respond when the real world presents the team with the unexpected.

Part of the solution to the problem of executing projects lies in finding a different approach to planning, rather than simply trying to "plan better." Clearly, if

12 (Drucker, 1974) Management, p 321

we want a different outcome, we must do something different.

Most planning is based on a "controls" model that makes it possible to estimate costs and identify the details needed to complete the project. But the granular level of detail that works nicely for accounting or a supply chain or in other contexts is not so good for project managers during execution. Furthermore, many plans assume that everything goes according to plan, and that there will be no variation. "Planning for success" is what one manager calls it.

Here's the problem. Between project planning and project execution, there's a gap—a wide one. Inside that gap, there are conflicting priorities and a plethora of details to juggle: managing the many tasks in progress, reconciling the functional roles of project team members to the project objectives, identifying and mitigating risks, "surprises," and bottlenecks that block progress, and much more.

Typical planning approaches simply do not compensate adequately for the inevitable changes that take place during execution. Project managers continue to point to poor estimation during the planning phase as the largest (32 percent) contributor to project failure.[13]

13 PriceWaterhouseCoopers, "Insights and Trends: Current Portfolio, Programme, and Project Management Practices," 2012.

The typical planning approach, however, does not do well in managing the uncertainties that can impede on-time delivery, and the task estimates that compose the plan *can't* be accurate without factoring in uncertainty. Additionally, the Work Breakdown Structure, or WBS, used as a foundation for planning is linear and hierarchical—it doesn't reveal or account for the dependencies, sequences, and "handoffs" among plan elements. While "good planning" does define the work, it doesn't define the relationships, or—just as problematic—it attempts to define *all* of them.

The relationships, however, are precisely what need to be managed during execution.

Managing a plan with too much detail creates a needle-in-the-haystack situation that slows decision making and action. When the level of detail is right, project teams are able to anticipate the consequences of any change; but when projects are overplanned, consequences are impossible to forecast and the team is incapable of responding effectively. They become, to borrow a metaphor, lost in the forest, unable to find the right trees. As problems arise, the team struggles to find a way toward a solution, unable to clearly see the right course of action. To compensate, project meetings become long, tedious affairs in which everyone talks about what has happened and defends their actions to deflect blame.

Just as no one would advise commencing a project without planning, I am not advocating planning without considering the details. There is, however, a *right level* of detail: only as much as you can truly manage. This can be found by making a distinction between plans for control and plans for execution; these plans have different objectives and are created and deployed differently.

Forget Plans—Focus on Plays

"Inadequate planning" often really means "*over*planning." Just as often, though, "inadequate planning" means "inflexible planning." In reality, project problems are not so much a possibility as an inevitability. Things go wrong, and the more elements there are in a plan, the greater the likelihood that small issues will lead to bigger ones. Trying to manage all of the small details will eventually overwhelm any manager's ability to grasp the larger issues at hand. That's why more planning by itself can never lead to timely and efficient project completion. Burdened with details, complex plans become boa constrictors that squeeze the air out of the project, suffocating hopes for success.

The path to success, therefore, is not more planning, but *different* planning—planning focused on effective execution that anticipates uncertainty and has the flexibility necessary for addressing it.

Consider the sport of soccer (more commonly known as football outside of the United States): No amount of planning can guarantee success on the field. In fact, rigid adherence to a plan will hinder a coach and his team, not help them. Like the project manager, a coach needs the ability to implement plays that are appropriate to the fluidity of the situation, and to change those plays at a moment's notice. This is what will help him and his team win the game.

Whether you're coaching soccer or running a project, in order to succeed you need:

- **A clear view of the situation.** Can the team see what is critical to the status of the project? Successful coaches and managers make the game plan, the work, and the obstacles visible. When the project flow is clear to the team, they're able to direct time and effort to the smaller subset of activities that contribute meaningfully to the project goal. When the team members can focus on those smaller details, a project manager is able to focus on the bigger picture. For example, if you're the coach, you likely don't need to be nitpicky about the technique of your players; instead, your efforts will go toward making sure the right player is matched to the situation to execute the game plan.

- **Common goals.** There is no room in the game plan for individual players padding their statistics when you're trying to win as a team. Success demands perfect alignment and singularity of purpose among all team members. As in a football game, a project has no such thing as a "balanced" scorecard. Just as more blocked goals do not make a winning team, individual productivity and functional success are a part of project success, not a prerequisite to it.

- **Collaboration.** The team must agree on the general strategy of action and their roles in it. Instead of pursuing individual agendas, the team members cooperate to achieve their common goal through transparent communication, responding to the situation on the field and working the necessary next steps for moving the game forward.

Planning should not be discarded. But a plan isn't an objective in its own right. Its sole purpose is to enable and guide execution. Good planning makes that key distinction between control and execution. A project manager knows the right level of detail to manage, anticipating uncertainty and risk. To play the field that's in front of her, the project micromanager plays the hypothetical field she drew on the whiteboard before the game. By substituting dynamic execution for static compliance, you will acquire the power to make your workflows *work*.

CHAPTER 3

Do Your Team Members Know What Everyone Else Is Doing, or Are They Alone on the Pitch?

The Importance of Visibility and Accountability

On a foggy day in November, a football game unfolds. The weather is a problem, though. The field is blanketed in fog and the left midfielder can't see any of his forwards. How will he know where the ball is or where he should direct his plays in order to support his team? How can he effectively do his job if he can't see what the team needs? When the fog shrouds the field so much that the coach himself can't see the players, how can he direct them to victory?

The same problem exists in projects. As the executive from chapter 1 told me, "I do not know where we are, or if we are in trouble or not." She didn't know what her team was doing, and so she couldn't ensure that they were going in the right direction, let alone guide them toward the goal. Simply put, **you can't manage what you can't see.**

When a project manager can't see the actions of the team, it's likely that the team members themselves don't know where they're going, where they are in the project, or what they need to get their share done. Team members don't know where they stand in relation to the project's ultimate completion, and so they are unable to act in ways that accelerate the project's progress.

The lack of visibility affects the team's ability to work as one cohesive unit. There's no way for the team members to leverage their strengths, and the synergy of the team is limited. The first and main obstacle to improving visibility is the sheer volume of work. Too much work or too many tasks in the system obscures the playing field. There is simply so much of it that the team cannot sort through it all to identify the most important tasks to concentrate on.

Another obstacle to achieving situational visibility is the inability to see the progress of the work. If you're working on an intangible deliverable, like software or design, all you can see is your people at work at their desks, on the phone, on the computer, or in meetings. But what about the work deliverables? What's their status? How can you know?

Of course, it's hard to know. You walk down the hallway and you can see people busily engaged with their computer screens. You naturally want to assume that they're working on project tasks, but the truth is, you have no way of knowing what they're doing. Even if they're not on Facebook or on various Internet discussion groups, how do you know specifically what they're working on, or what their status is, or if they're directly helping the ultimate goal? At best, you might have a rough idea—and rough won't cut it.

Due to the lack of visibility in the workflow, you don't know where the problems are, where to focus, what to prioritize, or whether your team's work is on time or not. (Unless they're already late. Then, of course, everyone knows.)

The primary problem in project execution is that the teams simply do not have situational visibility. They can't see where they are, and they can't see clearly what to do. They do not have a useable map to guide them.

So how do the teams respond? They have a meeting, and then another meeting, and then another to try to figure out where they are and what's going on in the project and what they need to do. The problem is, no one on the team has a complete picture of the project. They're like the blind men describing the elephant, each one describing what they "see," but none of them getting a complete picture of the entire animal.

Then there are the project "reviews," in which everyone talks about what went wrong and why that deadline wasn't met. Questions are asked *in hindsight*. The problem is, hindsight is 20/20. Executives are managing problems that have already happened instead of looking ahead to establish what needs to be accomplished to *prevent* further problems. Often these meetings are exercises in finger pointing, and the environment takes on a culture of blame rather than one of cooperation. Accountability is avoided and falls to the wayside, because no one knows who was responsible for which detail to begin with.

We know that planning is not the leverage point—execution is. Without any plan at all, though, team members are left to execute on their own. Team members can see the big picture in general, but the path between their individual tasks and the project's ultimate success is lost.

Seeing through the Fog

In order to create a mutual awareness and alignment of action, make what is meaningful **visible**. Visible information is the shortest route from understanding to action. Brain research shows that we decipher visual information simultaneously, whereas language and text are processed in a sequential manner.[14] Having a visual aid significantly reduces the time needed to understand information, thereby promoting rapid understanding of any situation. You need a map.

Media theorist John Berger writes in his book *Ways of Seeing* (Penguin Books, 1972), "Seeing comes before words. The child looks and recognizes before it can speak." Lynell Burmark, PhD, associate at the Thornburg Center for Professional Development and expert on visual literacy, agrees:

"Unless our words, concepts, [and] ideas are hooked onto an image, they will go in one ear, sail through the brain, and go out the other ear. Words are processed by our short-term memory, where we can only retain about seven bits of

---

14 Parkinson, Mike, The Power of Visual Communication, http://www.billiondollargraphics.com/infographics.html

information (plus or minus two). This is why, by the way, we have seven-digit phone numbers. Images, on the other hand, go directly into long-term memory, where they are indelibly etched … Humans process visuals 60,000 times faster than text."

Presenters who use visual aids are 43 percent more effective in persuading audience members to act. Mike Parkinson, author of *Do-It-Yourself Billion Dollar Business Graphics*, says:

"Graphics do what text alone cannot … [graphics] affect us both cognitively and emotionally:

1. **Cognitively:** Graphics expedite and increase our level of communication. They increase comprehension, recollection, and retention … increasing the likelihood that the audience will remember.

2. **Emotionally:** Pictures enhance or affect emotions and attitudes. Graphics engage our imagination and heighten our creative thinking by stimulating other areas of our brain (which in turn leads to a more

profound and accurate understanding of the ... material)."

Increasing visibility within a team highlights critical information in ways that simply can't be ignored. There are many ways to create tangible visibility for the team; the solution our firm uses is the ViewPoint Visual Portfolio Board (VPB), which serves as the clear map that teams need. After a Colorado (US) software company instituted a VPB, an executive responded, "As simple as [a VPB] sounds, to actually see that come to life is a real clarifying moment for the entire organization. Everyone knows exactly where we are every day."

Having the right visual of your project exposes process problems to the team in an objective, non-threatening way. A clear visual also prevents information overload. As the project continues, a visual like the VPB provides tangible feedback that everyone can see and understand. The VPB removes the largest obstacle to collaboration: agreement on the situation. If there's a bottleneck or a gap on the board, team members don't waste time arguing about it because it's obvious there's a problem. They know where they are. Rather than working toward an unclear goal, members of a team can monitor the project and take the right action to move it closer to completion.

A Shared Purpose

When I look at many project teams, I see they don't function as a team; they don't have this same idea of mutual accountability to achieve a common goal. In many organizations, there is only one person who has the goal of getting the project done—*one* person, and that is the project manager. Somehow, he has to take this team of people—selected from various functions and organizations to execute this project—and make them accountable to the single goal of completing the project. And when I look at what project managers are doing, I see that this is where they're spending most of their time.

Project teams typically consist of people skilled in various disciplines: technical experts, operations experts, subcontractors, supply-chain managers, financial controllers, schedulers, etc. Each of these team members is placed on the team to accomplish the project's objective, and yet they each bring with them the objectives for their functional discipline as well.

For example, you have the person who is managing people resources. She wants to keep everybody busy. If she doesn't, her measures will likely show that she has too many people. "Too many people?" some managers will say. "Inefficient! You must reduce your head count!" No one really wants to let their people go, so the resource manager and the people reporting to her have the objective of keeping busy—which, unfortunately, is *not* the same as completing the project quickly.

And then there are the team members who say, "Well, we must earn the hours. If we don't earn the hours, then we don't show progress and we can't get paid." And then we have the controller who says, "Well, we've got to stay within the budget. You've only earned this much, so you can only spend that much."

The conflict in purpose is built into the system. Shall the team members submit to the project's objectives, or to those people who determine their paycheck? It's unlikely they'll commit fully to the project. As a result, the project team will be plagued by conflict and will behave in ways that don't contribute directly to accelerating progress toward a common goal. No wonder project management is sometimes referred to as "herding cats." None of these people on the team are really working toward the same objective.

How can you tell if your team is out of alignment? The things you should look for are a lack of responsiveness, low engagement with the project, and slow task completion or problem resolution. You may also spend a lot of time trying to find the person who's accountable for solving a particular problem, and you may find it difficult to obtain resources (from your "teammates") to support your project.

Making the project visible doesn't kill the conflict, but it does expose it. Building accountability starts with making the work visible. From there, the team members can create genuine accountability for action and a shared purpose. When the project is visible, no one can hide—and no one needs to.

Know Your Role

To be clear, *accountability* is not about discovering which team member made a mistake. Accountability is established by knowing who owns which area and what needs to be done in order for each individual to accomplish his or her personal goal in the project. Recalling our soccer team, in order to play effective offense, the team must move the ball out of the defender's zone and toward the opponent's goal. The goalie and his defensive team must clear the ball—and they have to clear it with a purpose. In an ideal world, midfielders will take up responsibility for helping to move the ball up the field, and once the ball gets into the attack zone, the forwards have the task of scoring.

Each player has a specific role and is accountable—that is, he is responsible for executing that role, thereby supporting the team's strategy. If the ball is in the defender's zone, a forward cannot and should not reasonably expect to go get it himself; nor does he likely have the capacity to elude an entire opposing team himself while he moves the ball up the field to score. A forward must trust his teammates to do their jobs effectively so that he can perform his—and in order to trust his teammates and carry his own weight fully, he needs to understand everyone else's responsibilities as well as his own.

Accountability creates team alignment toward a common goal. It encourages individuals to stretch their capabilities, and fosters mutual respect among peers. When accountability is present, team members are invited to do their very best—and raise their hands when they need help. Accountability encourages team members to focus on ultimate outcomes rather than on immediate activity.

The arguments for practicing constructive accountability are overwhelming. In his book *The Accountability*

Revolution, Mark Samuel says that "accountability means people can count on one another to keep performance commitments and communication agreements." According to Samuel, accountability can result in increased synergy, a safe climate for experimentation and change, and improved solutions because people feel supported and trusted. All these positive results, he says, raise employee morale and satisfaction (this is my experience as well).

The project team is just like the soccer team. Everyone is on the playing field. They should be able to see the players. They must see the ball. They must understand what they need to do. Everybody needs a clear understanding of where they should be on the field and what their responsibilities are, and they all must have the same goal of putting the ball in the net more often than the other team.

What we want to do is get our project team to function more like a real team, working together to achieve that goal.

CHAPTER 4

Murphy Lives!

Managing Uncertainty

If it can go wrong, it will.
—MURPHY'S LAW

Projects are inherently uncertain. Heck, life is uncertain! Surprises can come from any angle, and there often aren't enough resources on hand: A manager is taken aback by the larger scope of a project that he thought would be much less complicated; the weather is terrible; the supplier is late; the customer changes his mind. The list goes on. We can't predict with much precision how long project tasks will take, or whether things will work the way they're intended to. If it can go wrong, it will, and this means it's imperative that project managers factor uncertainty into their management strategies.

From an execution standpoint, we should not be surprised that Murphy lives. Experienced managers are not surprised by Murphy's law, so it's built into their process. Often, however, the approach to managing uncertainty is the solution that is so common to project management: "better" planning. Managers frequently think, *If I can imagine all the things that can possibly go wrong, I can plan for them and prevent them.* Unfortunately, there's no telling exactly what will happen or when, and plans must be made, as we now know, for flexibility in execution rather than control. There is variability around known factors, but we must also realize that there is variability around unknown factors as well. Managing uncertainty (or variation, as we'll sometimes refer to it) is about managing the expectations of outcomes.

There are two general kinds of uncertainty: *normal variation* and *abnormal variation,* also known as common cause and special cause, respectively. Normal variation is, simply put, normal. It's always present, always having its effect. For example, let's assume Sarah is going to the store before she heads to the office for a meeting, and the planned duration of her trip is half an hour. If there's traffic, or if the store is crowded, or Sarah can't find parking, that's normal variation, and it might take her forty minutes instead of thirty (a ten-minute delay is generally not a problem). In the long run, she is still likely to be on time for her meeting, even though she may be hurried or slightly unprepared.

Abnormal variation (or special cause) is unpredictable, however. Sarah gets on the highway to go to the store, and there's a train wreck that blocks the highway and leaves her sitting in traffic for hours. Or Sarah goes to the store—and the roof caves in. She's late for her meeting, or she doesn't make it at all, and then her role at the meeting isn't filled correctly and her work is affected. These are abnormal variations for which there is truly no planning.

I'm highlighting the difference because there is a certain danger in confusing the two types of variation. Unless we recognize that common-cause variation is always present, we will be overly optimistic or pessimistic in our plans. Additionally, if we fail to make this distinction, we will apply the wrong tools, fooling ourselves into thinking that we have done a proper risk analysis.

The PMBOK® doesn't distinguish between the two causes, and managers seldom consider variation in their decision making. A common coping mechanism employed when a task is delayed due to normal variation is to change the course of the critical path in an attempt to regain control, which doesn't necessarily help. In fact, it increases the likelihood of more variability.[15] If management treats abnormal variation as normal and does not change the course of action—if Sarah proceeds with her life as if the roof of the store hadn't caved in, and ignores the effect that her delay might have on a meeting she has later—the entire project is at risk.

Uncertainty's Impact on Project Plans

When projects exceed their time and budget allowances, mismanaged uncertainty is always a major factor. One way to manage uncertainty is to be very deliberate about duration estimates and who makes them, how they make them, and the amount of weight given to any estimate. Typically, each player in a project provides a project manager with a duration estimate that factors in both a reasonable prediction of the time needed to accomplish his or her task *and* some extra time (contingency!) as a buffer in case the task is more complex than the most optimistic estimate might suggest (Murphy lives, after all). People do not want to break their commitments. When the sheep are late coming in from the pasture, the shepherd is held accountable.

---

15 Leach, "Putting Quality in Project Risk Management; Part I: Understanding Variation," 2009.

Shepherds don't like to be hit with their own crooks, so they make conservative time estimates to allow the very last, fattest, oldest, slowest sheep to meander back from the pasture.

Aggressive, But Possible

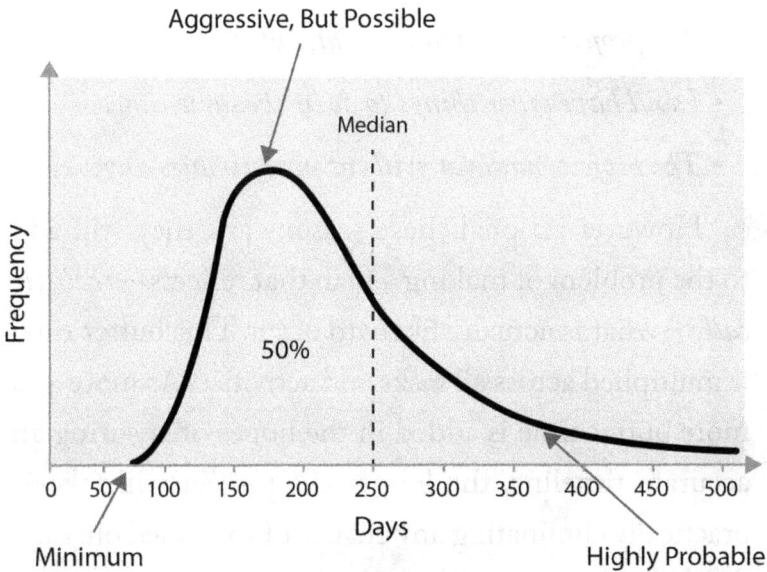

Seasoned managers do understand that task variation exists. Task durations don't follow a normal bell-shaped curve of probability for completion times; they skew toward the longer end and have long tails. In the curve of probability shown above, you can see that although the most frequent (and likely) occurrence is found at 180 days, there's only a 50 percent chance of finishing a project or a task at, or before, 250 days. In planning, people often are inclined to consider their very worst experiences when estimating the duration of a task (and reasonably so), so they add a buffer of safety time to ensure that they can meet their commitments. There are rational reasons:

- *The project will already be late when it gets to me.*
- *I will have other things to do at the same time.*
- *The project manager will cut my estimates anyway.*

However rational these reasons are, they still add to the problem of making a plan that reflects—*realistically*—what is actually likely to occur. This buffer time is multiplied across all tasks and activities. As more and more buffer time is added in the hopes of ensuring an accurate timeline, the longer the project will take—practically eliminating any chance of a planned on-time finish for the project. (For this reason, senior managers often cut project durations to fit the commitment or requirement of the customer.)

I want to highlight for a moment the most frequently cited reason for long task estimates: "I will have other things to do." In many organizations, the amount of work in the system (Work in Progress—WIP) is very high. These task estimates often compensate for the effects of too much WIP—people cannot imagine a world in which they are not multitasking and waiting for complete information, thus they assume a certain kind of execution environment that may or may not be valid. In other words, they may be right! Look to chapter 10 for a more complete treatment of this issue.

The problem is that nearly everyone uses this method to estimate the duration of the project. Consequently, a project manager with a hundred different tasks along the critical path will find it impossible to know what portion of his team's duration estimates is devoted to actual work and what portion of it is the team members' contingency time. Once again, we have a lack of transparency and visibility preventing the project team from making the best possible decisions.

Uncertainty's Impact on Execution

The task estimation dilemma isn't just about making a good plan; inflated task duration estimates affect how projects are executed. A common side effect of inflated duration estimates is that team members, knowing the planned durations are longer than necessary, are easily diverted to work on other tasks. When a due date is two weeks away, it's easy to set aside a task in favor of solving something more pressing or attractive. Once the task has begun, however, statistical variations crop up, and then even that buffer time that was originally allowed for is lost.[16] Additionally, early task completions are rarely recognized or rewarded. If a task is completed early, team members will often use the surplus time to polish their work, or even to take a break.[17]

It's also necessary for a manager to assess how much weight he or she gives to a particular duration estimate. If one task isn't completed on time, will the manager allow that to stop the entire project, thereby pushing back the deadline? Project managers hope—and often assume—that tasks that take longer than originally estimated will be offset by tasks that take less time, or that the schedule float will absorb them, but that's rarely the case. When tasks on the critical path exceed their anticipated timelines, more time has to be added to the overall project's duration in order to compensate. Inevitably, delays cascade through the project.

The most important thing for managing variation is separating the actual work duration from the duration for safety in the overall time, and managing them as separate entities. In chapters 12 and 16, we'll examine in detail a number of ways to manage uncertainty so that you have the tools to cope with schedule risk—and get your projects in on time.

---

16 This is called the "student syndrome."
17 Parkinson's law

CHAPTER 5

What about the Resources?

The Evils of Multitasking

You want to reduce your spending on your project? Stop wasting your people's time. My experience is that as much as 50 percent of your capacity is wasted. Lost. The biggest productivity loss, and thus the biggest loss of opportunity, stems from one thing: team members multitasking. Most people think that multitasking is a good skill to have—chewing gum and walking, reading and breathing, catching up on customer calls while heading to a meeting—and in these contexts, it is! However, when it comes to accomplishing actual work, research shows just the opposite. Managing more than one mental activity reduces the brainpower available for either task.[18] Distributing your attention among several activities taxes the brain, and comes at the expense of real productivity.

When we use the word *multitasking* in the workplace, what we truly mean is "rapid task switching." In a nutshell, this means stopping a task before it's been completed, then taking on a different one.

Everyone does it, this task switching. How many times have you gone into work and sat down to write an e-mail, only to receive a phone call from someone who wants you to e-mail them a document about something else? You abandon the first e-mail, send the second, and before you can go back to your initial e-mail, your boss comes in and asks you to work on a new task.

The Problems with Multitasking

In short, multitasking adds work—hidden work—to your project in two ways.

The first is that multitasking robs our people (and us!) of cognitive ability. Research shows that we lose quite a bit of our ability when we're dividing our attention among multiple activities, causing up to a 40 percent decline in productivity. To perform complicated

18 Just, "A decrease in brain activation associated with driving when listening to someone speak," 2008.

tasks, you need to slow down or you'll make mistakes—
and if you're multitasking, the tasks will take even longer
than they should.

But that's just how it affects individuals. There is
another, more important effect that managers must
contend with besides slowed progress: the creation of
additional, unplanned tasks. In a way, managers inadvertently create more work and then punish their people
for not keeping up (I can hear the cheers now!). Most
of this work comes from two sources: additional setup
time, and sequencing delays. I know a delay isn't technically more work, but bear with me. The good news
is that since managers can create extra work, they can
stop creating it.

Switching back and forth creates unplanned work in
the system, which can only add time and complications.
Let's consider the first source of unplanned work: additional setup time. For any task, there's a certain amount
of setup time required before you can begin doing the
real work. To restart a task, you must review the work
you've done, determine where you left off, and then
decide what to do next. The more complex the task is,
the longer the setup time required to resume it—and
the more switching you do, the more setups you'll do,
and your project will inevitably take longer.

Another dimension of multitasking is quality. When people multitask, they make mistakes—which then adds more time to a project as they work to correct those mistakes. The unplanned time spent on a task increases as the complexity increases.[19] When there's more work that wasn't initially built into project plans, there are more unanticipated delays and an increase in unplanned resource requirements (load), and thus, costs.

Secondly, let's look at sequencing delays. Consider tasks on the critical path. Tasks are dependent on prior activities and must be completed in order—A, B, C, etc. When the deliverable produced at task A appears later than expected, task B is delayed from the start, then the overall project is already delayed.

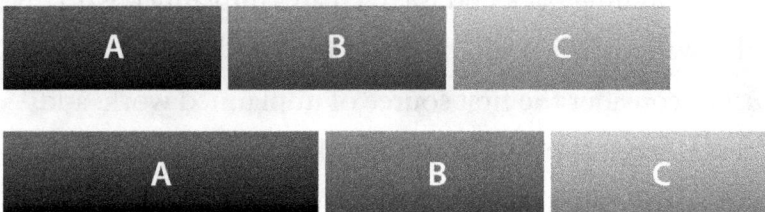

That basic delay isn't the only effect. Since task A is late arriving, the person assigned to work on task B has moved on to a different task because they couldn't begin task B without having the deliverable task A produces.

19 Shellenbarger, "Multitasking Makes You Stupid, Studies Say," Fort Worth Star Telegram, March 1, 2003.

When task A does arrive, the team member isn't going to drop their new project and begin task B; they want to finish what they're doing. Task B then gets further delayed because there is now an extra contender for that person's attention—and task C that might follow task B is delayed in starting as well. Eventually, the person responsible for task B can start the "correct" task, and the cycle starts again, cascading delays through the entire chain of project tasks. Depending on the length of that chain, the whole project could be delayed far longer than the length of any single task delay.

Multitasking has an effect that is unique to project work: task coordination losses—that is, the inability of the team to keep up with scope changes, clarifications of customer requirements and debates about the scope, some of which don't turn out the way many team members assumed they would when they began their work. Responding to these changes means *more* delays and rework that accompany multitasking. The more dispersed the team, the more often this happens. Multitasking makes what would be a normal coordination problem, actually delivering against those requirements even more difficult to tame. As a result, the team could be working (maybe even productively) on incorrect scope, not just a team working unproductively on correct scope.

This additional work caused by multitasking requires more people, which in turn drives costs higher. The worst thing is that these delays are hidden from the project team, and the problem creeps up on them. They aren't really able to see it because of the visibility issues I discussed in chapter 3—that is, until the project is seen to be late, which then triggers all sorts of expediting activity, again increasing costs for the entire project. Poor planning is certainly a killer of projects, but multitasking is the most common cause of delays and poor budget performance, and it affects *every* project.

If multitasking is so bad for our productivity (and our projects), then why do we do it? Surprisingly, it is not because people like variety. Multitasking can be attributed to four major causes: bad priority signals, bad measurements, too much work in the system, and incomplete work in the system.

Which Signal Do I Follow?

Imagine that you have ten different tasks on your desk. How do you choose which one to work on right now, assuming they're all ready to go? Is there a sequence you should follow? Do you choose what you like? Does your boss tell you? This is the problem with prioritizing. If it's just you, or maybe a handful of people, you'll find a way to muddle through. But when you're leading a project with hundreds of people in different locations who are working with complex task dependencies, setting task priorities is important to ensure that the project is moving forward—ensuring that the right work is being done *today* to advance your project.

There are several priority signals that people will follow—and none of them are good for your projects:

- *The Squeaky Wheel Gets the Grease:* Whoever calls most frequently or makes the most noise gets top priority. This may be a result of project meetings and a particular leader's understanding of what has to happen next.

- *Flattery Will Get You Somewhere:* Everyone is acquainted with the "friend" who uses flattery and favors (beer!) to move their pet project to the top of the to-do list.

- *People Pleasers:* Instead of focusing on any one project or manager, a person tries to make everyone happy by applying a little bit of work to each project. Sometimes there's pressure to show progress on a certain project, even if that project doesn't seem to be most time-sensitive. Unfortunately, this ensures that these people will constantly be switching from task to task, which is appallingly inefficient and adds time to each project, increasing the sequencing delays.

- *Last-Minute Changes:* If we don't know where we are and where we're going, task priorities are going to be a rather ad hoc affair, with new priorities being created every time new information arrives. New meeting? New set of priorities! The customer is coming tomorrow? Everyone work on *that* project! The team itself creates its own brand of task switching.

The main point I want you to take away from this is that this switching behavior is far more often driven by management than by team members—meaning that it's up to the managers to resolve the problem.

Misleading Metrics

Numbers are never neutral. Management guru Eliyahu Goldratt famously observed, "Tell me how you measure me and I will tell you how I behave. If you measure me in an illogical way, do not complain about illogical behavior."[20]

Goldratt's point? People conform their behavior to the means of their measurement. In turn, managers get what they measure. For example, most people exceed the speed limit—*except* when there is a policemen or a speed camera at the side of the road, in which case nearly everyone slows down. The policeman gets almost everyone to change his or her behavior by simply measuring it with the threat of a certain (negative) consequence. In the context of project management, the call for data-centric decision making has given rise to a greater respect for metrics. But many people fail to recognize when they're measuring the wrong things—thereby encouraging the wrong behaviors and discouraging the right behaviors.

No mismatch between intention and consequence is as great as the one between cost and value. In an effort to control costs, many managers apply a resource

20 Goldratt, *The Haystack Syndrome,* North River Press, 1990.

utilization metric—a measure of "earning" per resource "cost." Tasks are assigned a value that is earned as they are completed. These earnings are then compared to the expenses necessary to create them. A positive ratio of earning to expenses generally means that the project is profitable. The problem is that the real value is not in an individual's output, but in their contribution to the overarching objective: completing projects that produce profits. By applying the cost metric of utilization rather than a value metric that assesses outcome, resources are "rewarded" for doing *any* work, not the *right* work. "Earning" value is not the same as advancing the project—especially when that "earned" value is off the critical path.

In order to keep everyone busy, managers create more problems by flooding the system with early work. Instead of encouraging work that advances the project, they are rewarding busywork. Earned value is a great way to budget, but in managing the execution of projects, it's a great way to hide the true status of a project.[21]

Be careful with what you measure. Rather than create metrics that track resource efficiency, apply metrics that reveal the behaviors that drive overall system

---

21 CIO Insight, "How to Lie with Earned Value," 2005.
http://www.cioinsight.com/c/a/Past-Opinions/How-to-Lie-with-Earned-Value/

progress and performance. In chapters 7 and 8, I'll give you some ideas.

Too Much Work in the System

It seems like common sense: Start sooner, and you'll finish sooner. The problem is that *everyone* starts sooner. Increasing the volume of the work in progress merely increases confusion and conflict—and decreases real productivity. Having a lot of work does accomplish the objective of keeping people busy. However, while everyone is busy, the true picture of the overall project is obscured until deadlines approach, and the failure to complete the right tasks becomes all too visible.

The more work you have stacked up, the more opportunities you have to multitask and to work on the wrong thing, doing tasks out of sequence or too soon. Which task should you prioritize? How many tasks do you have on hand? How many tasks *should* you have on hand?

The extra work complicates the priority-setting problem I just mentioned. If you have ten tasks on your desk and no guidance on priority, what are your criteria for choosing? Do you pick the task you're really interested in, or the task you don't understand that will require the most concentration? Do you pick the one with the closest deadline, or the one that you can finish the fastest?

Most of us will automatically choose the task that is most interesting to us. Unfortunately for those of us who get bored easily, this has as much of an implication for projects as delays do; if the wrong task is picked to be worked on, then the wrong work gets introduced into the system. Visibility can help this issue—if you can see what the other team members need from you in order to push the project forward, then you can prioritize accordingly. But without visibility, there's no way to know which task you should start with. The right work lags, and the wrong work moves ahead. Once again, the next link in the chain will move on to a different task instead of waiting to receive the completed one they need—and the delay cascades down the chain, growing exponentially again. The project team gets loaded up with work that shouldn't be in the system, and then there's expediting and sorting to be done for a project or process that shouldn't need it at all. Then we're back to multitasking, and the process begins all over again. It's a vicious cycle—one that creates extra work for the team members and additional management overhead to deal with it.

Just as adding more cars to the highways doesn't mean everyone gets where they're going faster, putting more work into play will never accelerate progress. Starting more work does not equate to finishing more work. Starting more work means finishing *less* work.

False Starts

Adding more work will not lead to more accomplishment, and similarly, rushing task initiation won't automatically lead to faster project completion. Under pressure to demonstrate progress, people will often start tasks before they and their teammates have all the information, designs, supplies, or tools they need to complete them (they have all this work!). These false starts are more than mere nuisances—they're obstructions with significant consequences:

- As partially-finished work clogs the workflow, *every* task takes longer and longer to fulfill.

- When team members don't have all the information they need, they make decisions based on only the available data, resulting in …

- Re-work. If the prior assumptions were incorrect, partially completed work then will need to be redone, creating more unplanned work—which in turn causes additional costs and delays.

Multitasking needs to be treated as a systemic issue. Nearly half of American workers feel that they're *expected* to finish too many tasks at the same time.[22] Multitasking is the number one killer of productivity, particularly in knowledge-based projects like software or product design. What typically passes for project management is not, in fact, managing projects, but sorting and sifting through the work in the system and telling team members to stop and start. When project managers can control the amount of work in the system, help their team members prioritize their tasks, and assess productivity effectively, only then can the team members perform at peak levels.

---

22 Shellenbarger, "Multitasking Makes You Stupid, Studies Say," 2003.

PART II

Delivering Your Projects on Time and on Budget

CHAPTER 6

Introducing ViewPoint: Streamlined Project Execution

Visual Project Management and the Project Execution Maturity Model

Clearly, we need to rethink our success model and challenge the conventional wisdom about what drives superior project performance. The real-world results show that the conventional sequence of project management—make a good plan, then execute that plan, then *success!*—simply isn't working.

Instead, we can find the true leverage by placing execution practices at the start and using them, rather than the plan, as the foundation for success. To do this, we need a model of best practice.

In general, "best practice" or "maturity" models quantify the capabilities and practices that will deliver a certain result. Using a model, you can compare your organization's practices to the best ones, and assess what you need to be doing to improve. In short, a good maturity model is a tool that you can use to get better.

However, proven project execution methodologies are rare. Little research has been done for the purpose of developing a "best practice" for delivering projects. There's no one set of principles for managers to follow. In our research, we identified over thirty maturity models[23] based on various paradigms. Some are relatively well established, but in general, the maturity models most commonly used are not making the difference in performance that we want and need.[24]

Recognizing the *results* of project execution is easy, but the *processes* that create those results are difficult to see. In large and widely dispersed operations in particular, one cannot directly observe the behaviors of people and the processes they use to deliver projects. This makes it very difficult to recognize the things they're doing that yield specific results. Therefore, leaders cannot evaluate what must be changed to ensure that the team's actions will make a real difference in project results.

---

23 Brookes, "Using Maturity Models to Improve Project Management Practice," 2009.
24 Pinnacle Strategies, "Training and PMOs Will Not Save Our Projects; The State of Project Management Practice and Effectiveness," 2014.

Whatever model we use or create must deal, at the very least, with the three major problems we have in execution:

1. **Visibility:** During execution, the team doesn't know where they are relative to where they need to go; they're in a silo.

2. **Uncertainty:** We don't manage variation and uncertainty well.

3. **Capacity:** We are unable to integrate information about the availability of resources into project planning and project execution.

This model should also meet the following criteria for a solution. It must:

- Deliver fast, significant results;

- Be simpler than the current practice, with few obstacles to implementation;

- Adapt easily to different organizational cultures, regardless of current practice and project management process maturity;

- Work with and complement existing methodologies and software; and

- Generate maximum buy-in to the right practices, or at least generate no opposition.

A good project execution model should use the principles that drive on-time and on-budget performance. There must be a clear relationship, too, between those principles and the desired effects.

So what are the behaviors that exemplify those principles? Where is the path that takes your organization from where it stands now to a greater level of maturity, capability, and results?

The answers to these questions are found in the ViewPoint visual project management methodology, with which all detail leads to the end goal: execution.

ViewPoint Visual Project Management

The process of streamlining your execution capability begins with gaining control of all the work in the project delivery system. This may seem like a straightforward task, but when you have hundreds of people and thousands of tasks, gaining real control can be daunting.

However, once you have control, you can focus on execution tactics and strategies to end multitasking and reclaim that lost capacity. That capacity can then be used to accelerate your projects to deliver on time and on budget.

In short, ViewPoint offers three keys to successful execution:

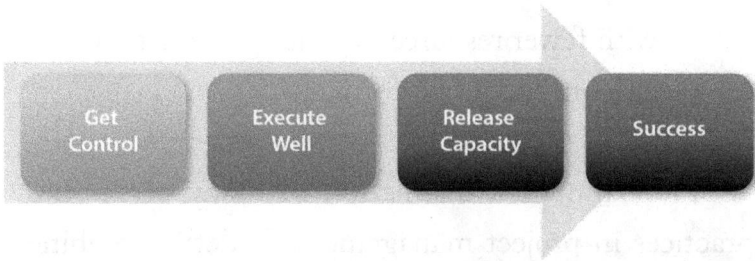

1. **Control the Work:** All of the work in the system is visible, and managed by the proper stakeholders.

2. **Intelligent Execution:** Team members direct their efforts toward the right tasks at the right times, collaborating as necessary to mitigate risk and ensure on-time completion.

3. **Release Capacity:** As a result of the prior two steps, capacity that was previously

consumed by multitasking and rework becomes available. You can then utilize that capacity to implement best-practice project management processes such as stakeholder engagement, risk management, and resource leveling, which all drive consistent, high-quality results. Your projects will be accomplished faster, and with fewer resources, resulting in on-time and on-budget performance.

ViewPoint is a distillation of many of the best practices in project management. It deftly combines the PMBOK® with Agile, Lean, and the Theory of Constraints to create a project delivery process that consistently outperforms customer expectations in cost, speed, and reliability.

Inherent in the ViewPoint method is an understanding that project planning, while important, is not the primary route to project success. Rather, it treats correct execution behaviors as the leverage point and prerequisite to significantly improved project performance.

The ViewPoint methodology utilizes a Project Execution Maturity Model (PEMM) that has been proven effective time and again. The PEMM is a set of principles and processes that, when followed, help managers identify and implement the best practices to drive superior results. Project execution no longer needs to be left to the artisans of project management; rather, it can be treated like a science, with clear cause-and-effect relationships between practices and outcomes. It doesn't have to be provisional or impromptu; it can be *taught*. In every country and culture in which we've implemented the PEMM (we have direct experience in Asia, Europe, and North America), the results are the same every time: expert execution and dramatic improvements in project results.

What Is the Project Execution Maturity Model, Anyway?

The PEMM is the foundation of the ViewPoint methodology. It provides a clear path from the very basic kinds of behaviors to more sophisticated kinds that create better results. It addresses the aforementioned issues with project execution (visibility, uncertainty, and resources) with three levels of execution capability: Basic Collaboration; Improved Coordination; and Integrated Planning and Execution.

Integrated Planning and Execution

| Probabilistic Planning | Capacity Management | Subcontractor Integration |

Improved Coordination

| Remote Collaboration | Managing Bottlenecks | Delivery Promising | Schedule Risk | Date Management |

Basic Collaboration

| Functional Alignment | Control WIP | Collaborative Execution | Priority Control |

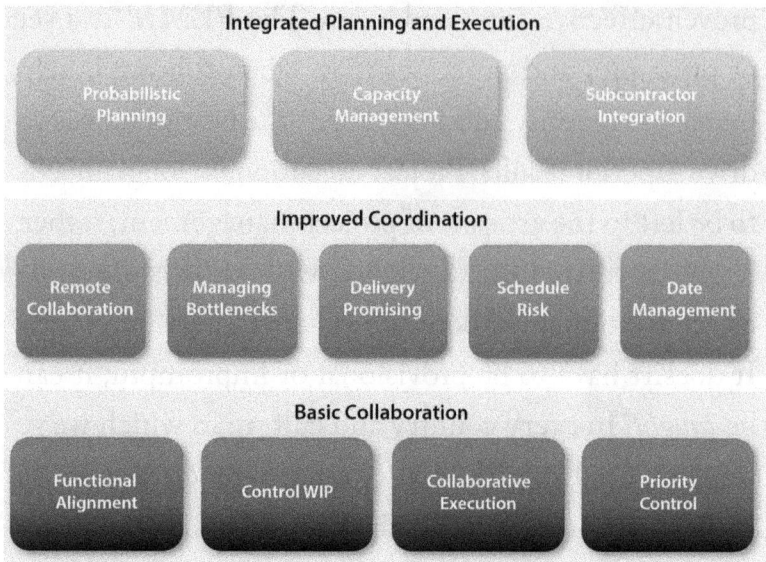

Each level of maturity is a reflection of the organization's ability to manage activity and time, extending from the "on hand" and "now" through the full life of the portfolio. In progressing through the PEMM, an organization will increase its productivity and effectiveness. By mastering all three levels of the PEMM, you'll find that your organization improves not only individual projects, but portfolios and the business as a whole.

Basic Collaboration is the foundational element of execution maturity, and it focuses on task completion velocity, or flow. It extends to a local work group or portfolio, and the timeframe managed extends to the completion of the tasks presently in progress. The major questions we look to answer at the Basic Collaboration level are: Can we get our work done? Can we get it done *quickly*? Can we effectively manage the work that we have in the system right now, and manage the team that we have at our disposal at this moment? Basic Collaboration addresses the short term: how to make what we have in front of us go *faster*.

Mastering this level of maturity will create a new reality for our project teams and set the stage for further improvement. We can then move on to **Improved Coordination**, which emphasizes meeting deadlines and milestone dates. At the Improved Coordination level, we'll also take the Basic Collaboration behaviors we've instituted and extend them to remote work groups. We're going to go fast, and we're going to deliver on time. Together, we'll also focus not only on tasks currently in progress, but on those that need to be completed in the near future, matching that future work with rough estimates of resource availability. Problem solving will extend beyond the work itself into dealing with resources and uncertainty. We'll go beyond the work that's directly in front of us, and start managing the work that will come later.

Once we've implemented the concepts in the first two levels and established a consistent pattern of good execution, we can then move on to the final level, **Integrated Planning and Execution**. Here, the focus is on managing risk across the portfolio at the task and resource levels, as well as managing risk that stems from subcontractors and suppliers. At this level of maturity, many of the traditional and non-traditional, more sophisticated methodologies of project management can be effectively used to truly close the loop between planning and execution. This, in turn, drives ongoing performance improvement. The PEMM guides the organization as it progresses from local, ad hoc execution behavior to integrated, *repeatable processes* that systematically deliver the superior results desired by team members, project managers, and clients alike.

Achieving greater execution maturity naturally leads to greater business value and results. Independent research, as well as our experience, shows that as organizations become more mature, they reap significant rewards, both in financial performance and in the success of their strategic initiatives.[25]

Simply moving from ad hoc to Basic Collaboration improves financial performance significantly, typically improving productivity by more than 10 percent,

---

25 Accenture, "Developing Strategies for the Effective Delivery of Capital Projects," 2012.

increasing the rate of task completions by nearly 20 percent, reducing overall project duration, and significantly improving on-time delivery performance—with similar gains as the organization moves to Improved Coordination and then to Integrated Planning and Execution.

Finding Leverage to Improve Project Performance

We know the results of execution, but again, the processes needed to lead a team to winning the game are often difficult to see. Using the PEMM, your organization can extract the full value from the investments you've already made in other project management disciplines and methodologies. ViewPoint and the PEMM utilize proven principles and techniques to drive on-time, on-budget project execution.

ViewPoint streamlines the process of executing your projects, improving team decision making and thus project outcomes. It provides clear situational awareness for all members of your project team, including those who govern the projects. The processes eliminate multitasking to improve productivity and shorten project duration. ViewPoint's methodologies give executives the ability to engage, resource, and focus project teams in a collaborative fashion—while providing visibility and accountability along the way. And perhaps most important, ViewPoint provides an executive governance structure for the portfolio of projects, providing focus and improving decision making for everyone involved.

In the chapters to come, we'll examine each of the three levels of maturity, and identify the twelve principles and practices that we've found effectively drive excellence in project execution. An understanding and implementation of these processes will give you a measurable means to assess your status, target the areas you need improvement on, and make tangible, meaningful improvements in the way that your organization delivers projects.

Stage One: BASIC COLLABORATION

Streamlining Your Execution for Speed

The first level in the Project Execution Maturity Model is **Basic Collaboration,** and it emphasizes task completion velocity and synchronization of your team's activities. We don't know where we are or where we're going, but Basic Collaboration will solve this lack of situational awareness for us. It answers the most fundamental questions of project execution:

- "What's the status of work in the system?"
- "Are we making progress?"
- "Is the project actually moving at all?"
- "Are the most important projects moving ahead of the others?"
- "Do we have the right resources deployed to the right tasks or projects?"
- "Where are the bottlenecks?"
- "What do we need to do to move forward, and who's going to do it?"

This level aligns your execution team by improving situational awareness. It also addresses the main causes of multitasking by controlling work priorities, and it indirectly mitigates project process variation by controlling the work in the system.

There are four major principles and processes to focus on: **Collaborative Execution, Functional Alignment, Priority Control,** and **Control Work in Progress**.

Basic Collaboration in Action

A leading provider of healthcare software was experiencing rapid growth, with the prospect of even more opportunities in their sales pipeline. However, the development organization was not fully prepared for this growth, and the current projects were at risk for late delivery.

They were using an Agile development process, with a software delivery team of approximately sixty people. While the process was flexible, the workflow proved difficult to manage. In the midst of rising customer demand for more software features, delivery could not keep pace with the workload. More and more developers were added to satisfy the rising expectations, but despite the team working long hours and spending many weekends writing code, nearly every promised delivery date was missed.

For the company, the stakes were high: By complying with new government regulations, their customer would be rewarded with grants and tax breaks—but only if they implemented the new program by its targeted date. Discouraged by delays and the lack of finished features, both the customer and the management were losing faith in the software development team. The organization decided to implement ViewPoint, beginning with the Basic Collaboration level.

The team members quickly realized that they didn't have visibility into all of the work in the system. Without visibility into the workflow, they had lost control of the delivery process. The ViewPoint framework complemented the Agile model that was already in use and supplemented it with formalized governance and management processes that would enable an increase in the number of feature deliveries.

The implementation involved:

1. Collaborative Execution: Without a "big-picture" understanding of the entire project, developers were working in the dark, blind to the collective goal. To create a foundation for collaborative action, they created a visual project execution process. Immediately, the entire team could see the "logjams" that required the most urgent attention. With simple, daily, fifteen-minute stand-up meetings, the team was able to effectively collaborate, rapidly identifying problems and removing obstacles. They were thereby able to dramatically improve productivity.

2. Functional Alignment: Before the implementation began, individuals and teams measured their progress in terms of their assigned tasks, regardless of impact on the overall goal. As part of the transformation, they realigned the entire development team with its collective objective: completing the final release for the client rather than completing individual features. Supported by the executive team, the execution team established new performance metrics that reflected the value driven to the client. These measurements facilitated increased productivity and improved software. In addition, the team reduced rework by introducing Clean Start requirements at critical handover points between project management and the design, development, and data/infrastructure processes.

3. Priority Control: The team created a tightly controlled priority system that reflected the global business focus and was used for all work. Priorities were set according to the feature sets that were most important to the client. The Priority Control system maintained consistency of task priorities throughout the workflow, aligning local priorities with the client's goals and commitments. This increased programmer productivity and practically eliminated rework.

4. Controlling Work in Progress: Like many teams under pressure, the team had started too many tasks at once, creating a "hurry up and wait" situation that clogged the workflow with unfinished work. Using the new Collaborative Execution process, the team selected a constraint—or pacing process—that dictated the delivery cadence for the entire workflow. By synching task starts to this constraint, the team limited the release of work in progress (WIP), which reduced multitasking and thereby increased the productivity of the entire team. As for the existing work, they froze 25 percent of the current active features and ensured that people (or teams) were not working on more than two features a day. This action served to restore flow and prevent the constraint process from being starved for lack of work.

In a continued effort to reduce multitasking and shorten project duration, they implemented a Clean Start policy and process and focused on *completing* the feature sets for which the team had full input requirements.

The result: Major Release completed by promised date with committed scope—and with less stress.

Within the first three months of implementing View-Point Basic Collaboration, the team *increased feature completions by 531 percent*. Additionally, there was significantly less stress and frustration among the team; thus morale was improved. The team met the next two major release dates, each time with less conflict, firefighting, and last-minute drama.

CHAPTER 7

Collaborative Execution

Developing Situational Awareness
and Responsiveness

When your project contributors lift their heads from their work and trade their individual cubicles for the conference table, what gets accomplished? Are your team's meetings a constructive part of the advancement of your project, or a discouraging exercise in placing blame? Simply put, is the team focused on the past or the future?

We know that in underperforming projects, issues are identified very late, and important communication is delayed. The right problem solvers are brought in too late to prevent the problems, and additional work—putting out fires—is then added to the work-flow. Capacity runs short, the project is delayed, and costs go up.

Superior execution requires informed collaboration, which requires both managers and team members to see beyond the limits of their individual tasks into the overall direction of the project. There can't be any dis-agreement about the status of the project or its priori-ties. The roles and accountability of each team member have to be clear—and everyone needs to know what has to get done *now*, rather than dissecting what happened (or didn't happen) in the past.

As we know, the lack of visibility makes project progress painfully slow. That lack of visibility prevents the team from choosing a clear direction and establish-ing accountability for action. Collaborative Execution kills much of the multitasking by addressing the lack of visibility and accountability.

The Collaborative Execution process answers the most basic questions about your project:

- "What is the status of the work?"

- "Are we making progress?"

- "What do we need to do to move the project forward?"

- "Who is going to do it?"

Making it Visible

We at Pinnacle Strategies find that making the work visible helps the full team see the large picture, as well as where their work fits into that larger picture. Football players have playbooks:

Movie producers use storyboards:

And for project managers and teams, our favorite tool is a Visual Project (or Portfolio) Board, or VPB.

The VPB is a physical representation of a project or portfolio that you and your team can see and track as projects progress—a map! The VPB helps teams see at a glance where the work is and where the problems are, so the group can act quickly to finish the work rather than using precious time to figure out where the problems are. The visual makes the final goal obvious to the team, facilitating alignment on the purpose of their work.

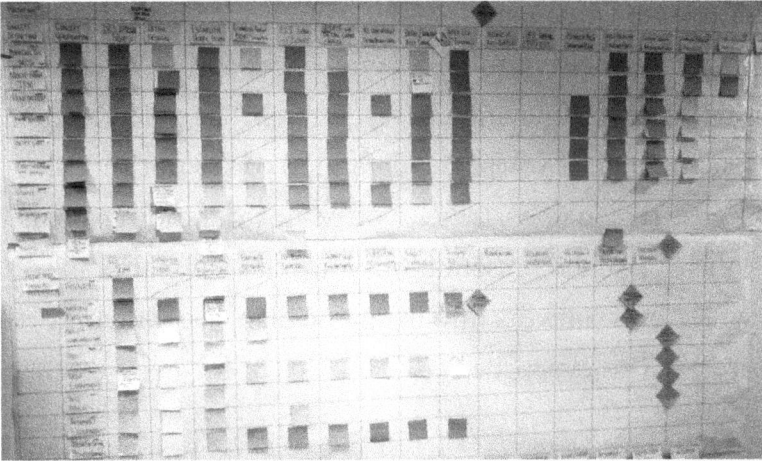

As the project or work progresses, a VPB (see example above) provides tangible feedback that everyone can see and understand. If there's a bottleneck or a gap, team members don't waste time arguing about where it is or whether it exists, because the situation is obvious. They know where the problem areas are. Rather than working toward an uncertain or ill-defined goal, members of the team can monitor progress and take corrective action early to move the right work closer to completion.

A visual representation of the process removes the largest obstacle to collaboration: agreement on the situation. Having a visual exposes and presents process problems in a non-threatening manner, and also prevents information overload. Finally, it facilitates the creation of an environment in which accountability can be established. Remember our soccer game? Everyone on the field is playing the same game, but not everyone has the ball. If you're the defender, you're not shooting goals. If you're a striker, you're not defending goals. With a visual representation, you and your team can see where everyone fits into the game plan; accountabilities are clear to everyone.

Building the Collaboration Structure

Now that you have a map, you need a clear set of rules governing collaboration. Collaboration is not an accident; it requires leadership and structure. Just like in any collaborative activity, you must have the rules and roles spelled out. To create a collaborative team, you must create an atmosphere of trust and accountability.

To foster collaboration, create a few simple rules to focus your team on what is *to be* done, not what *has been* done. History debates are for analysis, not Collaborative Execution. Consider and settle on the following: Who owns the board? Who owns the collaboration process? Who will facilitate it? How often do we meet? Who must be at these meetings? What will they do? Who has the handoff from one task to another? What happens if there are disagreements on the team? Who sets the work priorities? Who has the final word? Answering these questions will help you establish guidelines and structure to bring the right communication to the forefront and facilitate action.

Following some simple guidelines for Collaborative Execution will transform your teams. You'll find that:

- People are communicating regularly as a routine part of their work process. They won't just talk over coffee, but communicate deliberately about the work to be accomplished.

- Teams are focusing on what needs to get done for the project to move forward, instead of harping on the past.

- The team is engaged in everything, including problem solving. When challenges arise, the entire team pitches in to overcome them. Team members recognize that their individual roles and goals may need to take a backseat in order to ensure the success of the team.

- There are no "heroes," and you don't need them.

To elevate the quality of its product and its status in the marketplace, a producer of global positioning software implemented a problems and improvements (P&I) metric to monitor progress. Their initial P&I numbers proved discouraging: Progress was stalled by poor visibility of the work to be done and too many conflicting priorities, and these problems were exacerbated by the disconnect between customers in the field and software developers in the office. Software engineering efforts were constantly sidetracked by interruptions, delays, and a lack of consistent focus.

Pinnacle Strategies organized a Rapid Analysis Bottleneck Improvement Team (RABIT) to bring order, speed, and productivity to the software development workflow. Working with project leaders and software engineers, Pinnacle Strategies designed a Basic Collaboration process that had three crucial elements:

- **Master and monitor the workflow:** Within days of beginning the project, the team realized that the software engineers who were responsible for inputs from the formal P&I

workflow were being flooded with informal and unpredictable requests from the field. They quickly created a Visual Project Board to show all activity. The VPB became the centerpiece of ten- to fifteen-minute project collaboration meetings. Team members were able to improve the engineers' productivity, identify bottlenecks, and focus action on the most important tasks.

- **Establish a common contact:** To reduce multitasking, the team created a single point of customer contact: a toll-free number for field engineers to contact a single software engineer who had the ability to provide immediate support and the authority to make inputs to the task queue. Concentrating the contact function reduced support calls, e-mails, and visits to individual software engineers by 47 percent, thereby freeing up the engineers to focus on improving their software.

- **Create an FAQ page:** Too much time had been occupied by handling simple—and frequently repeated—field requests. The RABIT team built a frequently asked questions page within the company's intranet that reduced support calls, reduced interruptions, and improved field engineer access to searchable information.

Result: Resolution rates leapt from 0.5/week to 5.3/week.

In just two months, the organization was able to realize dramatic improvements in its problems and issues resolution process. Before they implemented ViewPoint, the average number of issues resolved in a week was 7.0; by the close of the project, it was 11.3, *a 61 percent gain*. Morale improved as well:

"The efficient daily five- to ten-minute meeting replaced the totally inefficient two- or three-hour weekly staff meeting."
—DEPARTMENT SUPERVISOR

Collaborative Execution is not an accident. By setting up the collaboration structure with simple rules, you'll have gone a long way toward improving situational awareness on your team. You'll be able to clearly see your obstacles and bottlenecks. Effective application of the principles will synchronize your team's work. It will also help your team identify problems early, improve team communications and engagement, and make your work go faster—with far less drama.

You'll know you have achieved maturity in Collaborative Execution when:

- The Visual Portfolio or Project Board is established and consistently used;

- Project team members are regularly collaborating to achieve project or portfolio progress; and

- The team is focused on the future.

CHAPTER 8

Functional Alignment

Working Toward a Common Purpose

Most project teams comprise experts from multiple disciplines: technical experts, operations experts, subcontractors, financial controllers, and the list goes on. Each of these team members is added to the team to help accomplish the project's objective—and yet each one also brings objectives from their individual discipline as well.

Few would argue against the value of goal-directed work. In most projects, though, the only person on the team with the single objective of completing the project is the project manager. The project manager, with limited organizational authority, must somehow sort the conflicting goals and still achieve the project's objective. Functional Alignment is necessary to get there.

Let's assume that the main goal for any project is the delivery of the chartered project scope. That scope has a set of concrete deliverables. There are necessary conditions as well, like cost and schedule, but the ultimate *goal* of the project is the completion of the deliverables. Now, for example, we bring the supply-chain leader onto the team. What is his goal? Is he automatically chartered to achieve the *project* goal? Typically not, as setting and achieving the team's project goal is the domain of the project manager, and the supply-chain leader has just arrived. Perhaps his primary goal, then, is achieving a favorable purchase cost variance. Unless someone relieves him of this responsibility, delivering the project is important to the project manager, but it's not the supply-chain leader's main goal—in which case we now have two people on the team whose goals do not match: the project manager and the supply-chain person.

Now let's add the financial controller. Is her goal to deliver the project? Just like the supply-chain leader, unless she has been relieved of some responsibility, her goal is likely to be budget compliance. Now we have three people on the team with three different goals. Every new party brings at least one new goal to the project. As I pointed out in chapter 3, you can't build collaborative teams without achieving unity of purpose.

The project team must therefore share a common goal and an understanding of the rules for working together. Team members must be able to make a clear distinction between the goal and the necessary conditions. When functional goals are aligned, each member of the team is free to act in the best interest of the project, without being hindered by conflicting goals from other areas. The team can truly begin to function as a team, working together to deliver results. Without alignment, your team will never get on the same page; the project manager's job will devolve from that of a coach into that of a referee. He or she will be forced to waste time sorting out internal conflicts while critical decisions are delayed, slowing the entire portfolio.

Functional Alignment increases productivity and reduces project duration by removing organizational friction from the project team. It reduces the time required to clarify accountabilities and obtain the right resources. It puts everyone on the project *on the project*, increasing engagement. That reduces decision delay while increasing engagement and facilitating productivity and the allocation of resources.

To combat the Macondo spill in the Gulf of Mexico, BP assembled the largest private maritime fleet ever, estimated at more than 10,000 vessels. Once the well was capped and the oil skimmed, though, BP was faced with a new challenge: decontaminating all the cleanup equipment and vessels—many of which they could not even find. In the haste to contain the spill, formal recordkeeping had taken a backseat to action. Many contracts and vessel identities went undocumented. Equipment was purchased, rented, leased, and used without any kind of comprehensive tracking process. BP was spending tens of millions of dollars to lease vessels each day, and millions more for the onshore facilities needed to support them. After the well was capped, the question became, "How can we get these vessels off the payroll as quickly as possible without sacrificing safety or the environment?"

Our firm's team went to work on solving that problem. Right away, they identified the bottleneck in the decontamination and decommissioning process: dock space. And the problem wasn't restricted to just one site; there were several sites around the Gulf of Mexico, from Texas City on the west to Miami on the east, a distance of over 1,100 miles.

As space became available, competing teams tried to cram their vessels in. Without coordinated reinforcement throughout the region, though, working spaces were blocked, occupied by boats waiting for specialty crews and equipment. While the cleaning crews waited for those resources to arrive, boats that could have been cleaned in that time idled in those working spaces, despite the fact that other working spaces were available elsewhere … while the payroll clock continued to run. This lack of coordination was a constraint on the process that led to an enormous amount of wasted capacity, delaying the entire project.

Tensions rose as different subcontractors with different objectives jockeyed for primacy. The decontamination team was undermined by distrust. So they made consistent, standardized performance communications and reinforcements a priority, not just to facilitate the workflow, but also to enable transparency among the team members.

Our firm's team, responsible for managing and communicating the performance of the overall process, designed a measurement and reporting scheme that emphasized utilization and productivity of dock space, thereby controlling the performance of the overall process. There were regular updates of constraint utilization, lost time, safety, and completions. These metrics provided a framework for management to understand the situation at remote locations and so facilitate timely decision making and action.

They then sent out teams to the various decontamination sites to establish local measures and reporting rhythms. Their efforts proved effective immediately, exposing the potential for a 50 percent increase in productivity. When this critical piece of information was shared up and down the chain of command, it created the impetus for action. Within days, dock utilization rose to 80 percent, then nearly 100 percent, with a concomitant increase in vessel completion.

"The effectiveness of the meetings and quality of information discussed in the briefings improved tenfold. The template for measurement and communications had a significant impact. If you increase the quality of the communications flow by 50 percent, you can easily increase throughput by 100 percent or more."

—DIRECTOR OF THE PERFORMANCE MANAGEMENT TEAM

In practice, this idea of Functional Alignment can be a bit nebulous. In most organizations I work with, I don't see big *conflicts* between goals very often; rather, what I see is an *absence* of goal alignment and guidelines that define good performance. There is really no context for creating alignment, so it's up to the project manager to define these goals and guidelines to get the team on the same page. And because project managers are not typically trained in this sort of thing, they don't recognize the problem for what it is, and the project suffers.

So—how do you do it? You're probably not going to change your corporation's measurement system. Rather than take on that monumental task, you need to implement ways to spot misalignment so you can mitigate or block it.

In order to establish Functional Alignment, you must determine what aligned behaviors you want, and then identify the existing behaviors that conflict with your goals. If you don't know what behavior you *do* want, look at what you *don't* want: Look at the unwanted behaviors and reverse them. For many of us, it's easier to see problems than solutions. This is not a perfect solution, but it's a place to start.

One shortcut to shaping behavior is to establish measurements and feedback processes. "Show me how you measure me, and I'll tell you how I'll behave."[26] So, to get your team aligned in their behavior, create and reinforce the right measurements.

In our projects, we start out with simple measurements to guide behavior:

- **Velocity**—The speed of task completion. Are we moving faster? Are we actually completing tasks and handing them off?

- **Rework**—How often do we have to do things over? The rule is: Always do it right. Don't sacrifice quality for speed.

---

26 Goldratt, *The Haystack Syndrome,* North River Press, 1990.

- **Frequency of Progress Blockages**—How often do we encounter surprises? The number of surprises we encounter tells us that people are not raising problems early—an important prevention behavior. We want team members to get into the habit of fixing problems as soon as they're identified. If we find an area that's at risk, or completely stopped, we want the team to respond.

These measurements are just starting points to align team purpose and behavior, but they're necessary. In assessing them, remember not to lose sight of the main idea—the team must have *one* goal, and your measurements will be useful to ferret out the conflicts and remove them.

When you've aligned the functions to the goal of the project, your team will at least have a foundation they can build upon to win. They won't be spending time resolving conflicts between your project and their own functions, and this alignment will speed up decision making and work completion. Functional Alignment promotes person-to-person teamwork and accountability, which in turn promotes faster project completion.

Organizations that demonstrate maturity in Functional Alignment show:

- A clear definition of the project's goal;

- Meeting the project goal as the main criterion for supporting team members;

- A distinction between the necessary conditions and the goal;

- A transparent process to achieve the goal;

- Measurements that reinforce the process behaviors to deliver the goal; and

- Metrics regularly presented to leaders who align near-term plans and activities to drive business results.

CHAPTER 9

Priority Control

*Keeping the Team Focused on
the Most Important Work*

As I discussed in chapter 5, managing priorities is one of your most powerful weapons to eliminate multitasking and boost productivity. Even with "formal" priorities, though, there's often significant disagreement among team members about what is the most important task to accomplish *now*. Priority Control reduces the duration of your project by addressing the primary cause of multitasking and killing unnecessary, unplanned, costly work.

We've all seen teams that can't decide on task and project priorities. Even worse are teams that have to live with multiple priority systems—one from the project management system, one from the enterprise requirements planning system, one from the manager, and yet another from their colleagues. It's no wonder their project meetings suck—no one can agree on what is the most important thing to do *now*, and priorities are determined by intuition and edict.

The result, of course, is that the flow of new information creates shifting priorities, which drive managers to constantly expedite, which in turns creates even more firefighting and more finger pointing. No one can get it right because there *is* no "right." Mistakes in task sequencing are made, so while the right work is being done, it's not done at the right time, and delivery commitments are missed.

Your Priority Control system maintains consistency of project and task priorities throughout the portfolio, for all projects. It aligns local priorities with goals and commitments that unite the efforts of the entire project team. It's transparent—everyone has an objective understanding of how priorities are set and changed, and what is the most important thing to do *now*.

By keeping a consistent priority scheme, the problems created by working tasks out of sequence are nearly eliminated, reducing cascading project delays. Task switching caused by multiple priority signals is eliminated, increasing productivity and speed, and reducing project lead times.

An airframe manufacturer had to expand production by 20 percent without increasing costs for labor, overhead, and inventory. While this was not strictly a "project," production of each unit was different, and production at any particular stage could take days.

In early 2012, their most important client had stepped up its production of airplanes, demanding an upstream increase in major assemblies—the bulk of the airframe construction—by 20 percent in the third quarter of the year. Under high pressure, they found themselves falling behind schedule. Finished products were not getting out the door at the same rate as component materials were coming onto the factory floor. This discrepancy in rates was costing them money—and threatening an important business relationship.

When our team members arrived to help, they quickly recognized an inherent contradiction between the objectives of the components supplier and the objectives of the final assembly department. In an effort to understand and manage the health of their execution process, the airframe manufacturer had created a metric that rewarded maximum output of each individual step in the process. While this focus did make it seem like each department was performing well, it had the unintended consequence of sacrificing the overall efficiency of the enterprise and failed to meet the true objective: to produce maximum value for the company as a whole.

A significant part of the solution was to realign the teams by changing the way they measured system health. They established a unified priority system. Multiple and conflicting priorities (hot, red-hot, and DO-IT-NOW) were causing chaos in execution teams, resulting in a "crisis mode" of management that robbed the system of productivity. The team created a transparent priority system aimed at the customer delivery due date—which aligned every member of the execution team with one common goal.

By implementing this and other elements of the execution maturity model, the organization improved their schedule compliance, and past due tasks dropped 40 percent in the first week of implementation. Improved performance led to less wasted spending on overtime to meet deadlines, and workers were assigned to centers where their contributions were most needed, which drove higher levels of productivity.

Your priority system need not be complicated, but it must be responsive to changing conditions and transparent to your team. If it's not, work will get done out of sequence, causing delays and lost productivity.

As an example of a simple process, we recently worked with a software development team in Norway. They created a simple prioritization number (PN) that ranked tasks by using category, severity, and business impact to determine priority. With the PN on hand, the team established task queues in sequence, making the priorities and the reasons for them clear to everyone. The PN was part of the solution that accelerated progress tremendously. Without priority confusion, the rate of feature completion increased almost tenfold— with the added benefit of pleasing the client when they received their releases sooner than expected.

Your Priority Control process can be as simple as this example, or it can take multiple steps and approvals.

The thing to remember is that the mechanism for establishing priority and the relative importance of tasks and deliverables must be transparent and deliver a consistent message about the order of work throughout the process.

In order to establish your Priority Control process, ask yourself the following questions: What are the criteria for setting priorities? Is it the final delivery date? A milestone date? The most important customer? The biggest boss? And just as crucially—who manages them?

A word about change and flexibility: You should not ignore reality and its impact on your work priorities; rather, you must recognize the fact that reality is changing. Therefore, you've got to have a mechanism in place to maintain clear priority signals when reality changes. That doesn't mean you should be inflexible, but it does mean that you should make sure that you can maintain the signaling mechanism when situations change. The priority system helps to create unity within the project teams and throughout the organization.

By establishing a transparent, well-governed priority management process, you'll eliminate the single largest cause of multitasking. This will improve team coordination, thereby shortening project durations, improving productivity, and reducing costs.

Maturity in Priority Control can be seen in organizations where:

- There is only one prioritization system that reflects the global focus, and it is used for all projects and supporting tasks;

- Project and task priorities are reconciled regularly among the affected stakeholders;

- There's a clear escalation process in place to resolve priority conflicts when they do occur; and

- Someone is accountable for establishing and managing portfolio, project, and task priorities.

CHAPTER 10

Control Work in Progress (WIP)

.Managing the Work to Increase Speed

Once we've set up the right structures for collaboration—
Collaborative Execution, Functional Alignment, and
Priority Control—we can move on to mastering control
of the work itself.

As I discussed in chapter 5, increasing the volume of
tasks in the workflow just makes managing everything in
the system more difficult. Management and team attention become divided, which prompts everyone on the team
to take up task switching before the work is fully completed. Each task switch and setup absorbs valuable time
and attention, adding work and duration to the project.

You'll have to deal with two aspects of controlling WIP:
managing the quality and managing the quantity—that

is, managing the content of what is released as well as the volume of work released into the process. Poor quality work creates too much stalled work in the system, and too much work just creates too much confusion.

Limiting Work in Progress

In earlier chapters, I wrote about the problem of too much work—it adds confusion, drives multitasking, and causes delays to cascade through your portfolio. These local effects are easy to see. This extra work is the hidden contributor to increased project durations and poor delivery performance. Therefore, it's critical for managers to monitor and manage the total amount of work in the system.

You must understand and master the practical application queuing theory known as Little's law, formulated in 1961 by John Dutton Conant Little. In the workflow context, Little's law can be summarized by saying:

$$\text{Average Project (Portfolio) Lead Time} = \frac{\text{Project (Portfolio) WIP}}{\text{Average Rate of Completions}}$$

OR

$$\text{Project (Portfolio) WIP} = \text{Average Rate of Completions} \times \text{Average Project (Portfolio) Lead Time}$$

So, if we are completing two projects a month, we multiply that by the average project duration of four months, for a total current WIP level of 8. Another way of saying this is that the length of time any given task will spend in the system is not only relative to the amount of work that task requires, but is also a function of the number of queues it encounters. Therefore, you can reduce your project durations by either changing the amount of work in the system or changing the completion rate.

When we introduce work into the system faster than the current completion rate, the project duration (queue) times increase. Aside from the wasted investment in idle work, queue times are important because they are significant to customers—they make the project duration longer.

Not only does too much work in our process affect customers, but it also makes your project and portfolio much more difficult to manage. When there's too much WIP, the priority system breaks down, resulting in extra work and resorting tasks. Managers spend all their time in meetings figuring out *what* the right work is, and then *where* it is. People (those who are responsible for doing the work) end up multitasking. It feels, and is, chaotic.

This chaos, this increase in management complexity, results in missed deliveries, lost customers, and eventually lost market share. You probably see these symptoms (complex management, priority-setting activities, figuring out where things are) every day, but you don't recognize them as symptoms—they're just accepted as "the way it is." However, your reality doesn't have to be that way. Keep in mind, though, that if you want to permanently eliminate the symptoms, you have to eliminate the causes.

A successful project or portfolio manager will have all three elements (completion rate, queue, and arrivals) well understood and under management. Limiting the amount of work in progress and controlling the rate at which work is introduced will accelerate the tasks remaining in the system and dramatically simplify the management and governance processes.

For this element, a simple way to control WIP at the beginning of your maturity journey is to freeze half of all projects that are currently in progress, and apply the freed capacity to more time-sensitive projects and tasks—and as each one is completed, others may be selectively "unfrozen." Of course, this is only a temporary measure to get control while you work out the mechanics of how to fix things permanently. If you're using a VPB, WIP is easily controlled by counting the number of cards in the system (as they represent work packages) or in a particular segment of the work process.

Clean Start

In addition to controlling the quantity, you must control the *quality* of work introduced into the system. The Clean Start process (sometimes called the Full Kit process) prevents work from being launched and then stuck in the process. It ensures that all the critical task or project *entry conditions* are met before you begin work. The Clean Start rule is simple: Don't start on something until you have everything you need to complete it.

The objectives of Clean Start are to reduce rework and delays (yes, rework is a delay, but we want to reduce other delays as well). It improves productivity by ensuring that only work that can be completed is actually started, so nothing starts and stops—no multitasking! Clean Start prevents the system from being clogged with work that cannot be sent along, and elevates blockages to higher levels of management for resolution (which is why this element comes *after* Collaborative Execution). It also has a nice side effect in that it eliminates overprocessing. Implementing the Clean Start process not only has the effect of reducing lead time and multitasking, but it also helps to apply pressure at the early stage of the project.

The Clean Start process has two components: a set of criteria for task completion and deliverables handoff, and a subprocess to manage all work that is in the "pre-release" state. In order to establish this subprocess for a task, managers must create and enforce transparent pre-release and handoff criteria for each step (as managed in the VPB) in the process.

This is all basic business process-engineering stuff, but for some reason, it has escaped the project management domain. We use the SIPOC (Suppliers-Inputs-Process-Outputs-Customers) process for each segment or step of the process to nail down the criteria. It's not complicated, and it doesn't have to be.

Managing the pre-release process can encompass a number of subprocesses, ranging from a very simple processes like managing checklists of requirements for release to complex change management and scope control procedures. The important principle to remember is that once the work is released into the process, progress never stops. Establishing a pre-planning stage for a "Clean Start" will pay you dividends by increasing productivity and reducing the duration of your project.

An engineer-to-order manufacturer of complex semiconductor machinery in Malaysia had many short projects (four to ten weeks), and the challenge was in managing the volume of projects (up to 150 in the portfolio) to deliver on time. Clean Start had an impact on their overall performance in two areas of the process.

The first was in design, at the beginning of the process. The design process was based on information provided by the sales team. Unfortunately, information was often not complete enough to proceed with the design of the machine. Typically, the engineer needed samples of the semiconductors to be produced in order to test the machine. However, the process for obtaining and managing them was rarely specified. Should the reject units be laser marked? How should the machine handle them? How sensitive are they to electrostatic discharges? What is the interface protocol with other equipment used by the customer, and what about other design dimensions?

Although delivery lead time was one of the most important buying criteria, the firm's customers were slow to finalize these important details. Usually the delivery date was established when the order was first committed. Thus, afterwards, when the customer was late in providing the needed information, the engineering team had to rush to complete these tasks by the committed date. This led to multitasking, rework, and lots of frustration.

The second area in need of improvement was assembly. Each machine is made of nearly one thousand components. Despite very good supplier delivery performance, they could never ensure that 100 percent of the components would be available by the scheduled start of the assembly process. Since delivery reliability and lead time were critical to customer satisfaction, employees were often rushed on the job, leading to multitasking and the associated loss of productivity.

A Clean Start (CS) procedure was implemented in front of each process. Clean Start One (CS1) ensured that all elements needed for the design were available before proceeding with the project. Since the customers supplied this information, the company changed their delivery terms to X weeks from CS1 completion. The Clean Start Two (CS2) process could not solve all the supply issues, but the company was able to use this process to shortlist the most important components that were required to be available. For both CS1 and CS2 policies and procedures, they created a checklist that was shared with the owner of the preceding task.

To sell these new processes and achieve rapid implementation, they suggested that the new CS policies helped to "spread" the big pressure from the end of the project to smaller pressure increments at various stages of the project:

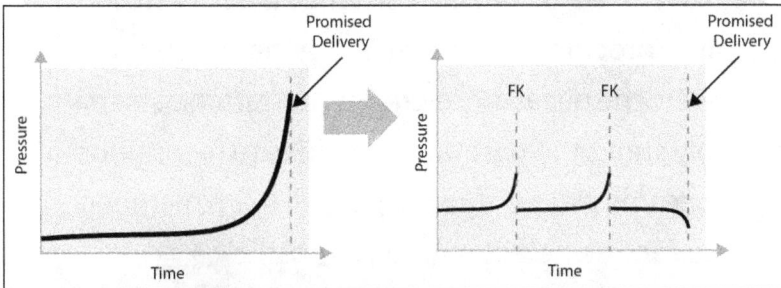

As expected, the owners of the preceding (delivering) tasks were unhappy about this new rule. Their tasks could only be closed after the CS checklist was completed, and so they were under pressure, despite the delivery date being far away. Although these workers weren't thrilled about the new pressure, creating the CS checklist saved time at early stages of the projects. This time turned out to be well appreciated later, as it eased the last-minute rush at the end stages.

That being said, the main success factor was support from management. The sales team had been pretending that customers were unhappy about the delays, but in fact, most customers were pleased to be provided with a comprehensive checklist at the very beginning of a project.

There was similar resistance from the sourcing (procurement) team. Yet by clarifying which were the necessary elements to start the assembly steps, the parts and activities to focus upon became clearer, thus helping all team members to focus where it mattered most.

"Before implementing the [Clean Start] process, we often heard from the supply-chain team, 'You have enough material to start.' Because the end of the project was still distant, they didn't feel any pressure to deliver every component required. Following

the implementation of Clean Start, [the supply-chain organization's] tasks were closed only when the next activity would have all material required to complete it. That increased the focus on them, affected their KPIs, and finally led to better performance. We have experienced the same scenario with sales representatives who needed to supply information about the project scope. The Clean Start policy helped to have clean starts."

—SENIOR MANAGER

In the end, they were able to increase production from twenty-five to forty machines per month, while holding less stock. The revenue followed this 60 percent increase, with virtually no increase in spending.

Getting control of your work in progress is foundational to doing anything further with resources or remote teams. After all, if you can't control what's in your own house, how can you help someone else get control of theirs? One of the underappreciated benefits of controlling WIP is that it simplifies the work of managing your projects. Less work in progress, less confusion. Less sorting. Less task switching. Less rework. All of this leads to a further reduction in project duration via improved productivity. You don't have to do things twice. Parkinson's law is negated. What's not to like? Get control of WIP!

Organizations with maturity in WIP Control:

- Have clear criteria for task and deliverable handoffs;

- Have a Clean Start or Full-Kit process to manage inbound work;

- Have established targets for total system WIP; and

- Have managers and leaders who meter the work into the system, staggering the release based on global priorities and resource loads.

Implementing a process to control your WIP:

- Simplifies task management and governance;

- Reduces project lead times;

- Reduces rework;

- Reduces project duration;

- Eliminates overprocessing; and

- Improves productivity.

Basic Collaboration Summary
Objective: Streamlining Execution for Speed

ELEMENT	BEHAVIORS	RESULTS
Collaborative Execution	• Visual Portfolio or Project Board established • Project team members regularly collaborate to achieve project or portfolio progress • Focus on the future	• Increased employee engagement • Situational awareness improves • Bottlenecks are identified and broken • Improved productivity, resulting in reduced project lead time
Functional Goals Alignment	• Regular reporting and analysis of operational metrics focused on process performance and end-project objectives • Functional or departmental objectives are subordinate to project objectives • Management takes an active role in governance activities	• Quick response to problems • Increased accountability for results • Reduced inter-functional conflict • Further increases in productivity, resulting in reduced project lead time
Priority Control	• A well-governed prioritization system • Priority reconciliation process (escalation procedures) • Clear accountability for establishing and managing priorities	• Improved synchronization of work • Improved productivity • Resources are applied to the right tasks at the right times

ELEMENT	BEHAVIORS	RESULTS
Control Work in Progress	• Have clear criteria for deliverable handoffs	• Simplification of management
	• Have a Clean Start or Full Kit process to manage inbound work	• Reduced project duration
		• Improved productivity
	• Have established targets for total system WIP	• Tasks can be quickly completed without delay
	• Have managers and leaders who meter the work into the system, staggering the release based on global priorities and resource loads	• There is very little rework
		• Task overprocessing is eliminated
		• Improved productivity

When you're executing multiple projects simultaneously, the problem identification and resolution found in the Basic Collaboration stage is critical for identifying and mitigating the unaccounted-for process variability (especially since you and your team don't necessarily have a "good" or executable plan). Additionally, without achieving a certain level of execution maturity, project managers will compete for resources, priority, management attention, etc. Breaking down the functional silos is critical in order to achieve consistent progress across the portfolio—so Priority Control and WIP

Control are essential to establishing and maintaining the integrity of the team's collaboration activities. In the end, project team members are not just members of a single project team; they are members of the *portfolio* (or organization) team. The principles and processes in the Basic Collaboration level of maturity establish and satisfy these conditions.

Once you and your team achieve maturity in Basic Collaboration, you'll see a significant increase in productivity. You'll also see reductions in project duration, which will drive an improvement in on-time delivery. As a result of the reduction in multitasking, you'll see a productivity improvement of at *least* 10 percent! All of the work in the system will be under control, and you'll know where it is, what the status is, how much is left, and where the problems are. Equally important, your *team* will also know these things. Everyone will have a clear view. Once you've established this basic foundation and are able to deal with the immediate tasks at hand, you and your team can then start to focus on the future, building on the work you've done so far, using more sophisticated concepts to address other dimensions of your process.

Stage Two: IMPROVED COORDINATION

Deliver on Time

Now that we've reached maturity in Basic Collaboration, we've gotten everyone's attention. Things are moving faster, but not fast enough. While our delivery reliability is improving, we're still not close to where we should be. Our team is still reacting to situations rather than anticipating problems. Even though we're getting faster, we still get surprises. We're spending too much money on schedule recovery efforts. Project durations have shortened, but not enough. The activity of our remote teams is not transparent to us. We still have work to do, and more steps on our journey.

The second level of project execution maturity—the next step up—is Improved Coordination. At this level, the emphasis is not only on completing tasks quickly, but also on reliably meeting delivery and milestone dates. Improved Coordination maturity also moves the team beyond local execution competence and extends execution capabilities to remote teams. The time and tasks under management shift from the present time (work in progress) to near future (up-and-coming work).

As with Basic Collaboration, when you achieve maturity at this level, flow and productivity will increase, but with additional management scope: a more sophisticated task and project priority system based on schedule risk, active management of critical capacity elements, and automation of critical management processes. More stakeholders are engaged, and progress accelerates faster. This level continues to eliminate the causes of multitasking, and directly addresses project process variation through simplified schedule risk and a systematic approach to managing critical resources.

Achievement of maturity in Improved Coordination answers more complex questions of project execution:

- "What's happening with our remote teams?"
- "Do we have enough resources for the work coming up?"
- "How can we be more proactive in resource allocation?"
- "How does new work fit into the existing work?"
- "Can we deliver this new work when it is required?"
- "What is the risk of completing late?"
- "How do we synchronize priorities within our IT systems?"

Within the Improved Coordination level there are five more principles and practices to master following the initial four principles of Basic Collaboration: **Remote Collaboration, Bottleneck Management, Delivery Promising, Schedule Risk Management**, and **Delivery Date Management**.

As your team achieves maturity in Improved Coordination, you'll begin to see:

- Dispersed teams that collaborate successfully and integrate with your "home" teams;

- Team members who understand each project's level of schedule risk and effectively work together to minimize that risk *before* it affects the customer;

- Teams that attack obstacles early to ensure project and portfolio success;

- Significant increases in speed of task completion;

- Shorter project durations;

- Improved on-time delivery performance; and

- Further productivity improvement.

CHAPTER 11

Remote Collaboration

Including Remote Teams in Your Process

If collaboration in one location seems challenging, then collaboration among far-flung teams in different offices—or different time zones or continents—probably feels impossible. Different locations cultivate different work cultures and loyalties, which naturally impede alignment and synchronization, and the potential for miscommunication increases with every additional mile separating team members.

With remote teams, you have all of the same challenges you had in your local team before you achieved Basic Collaboration:

- Work is done out of sequence.

- Resources are unavailable when needed.

- Work priorities are incorrect, and team members don't know what those priorities are.

- Resource overloads in remote locations will go unnoticed.

- The risk involving those teams is difficult to see and understand.

All of these have the same effect: slowing the project and increasing its duration.

When multiple teams are involved, and when those teams are dispersed around the state, across the country, or around the world, the effect on management complexity can be massive, inhibiting your teams' collaboration[27] in two significant ways:

- **Time Phasing**—*delays in communications.* When working across multiple time zones, there are delays in communicating critical information—task completions, blockages,

---

27 To be clear, when I say "collaboration," I'm not talking about the kind of brainstorming and relationship building that is critical to building effective teams. In the context of this discussion, I assume that the team is reasonably functional and that we have one purpose: Deliver the project or portfolio of projects on time and on budget.

quality problems, opportunities, etc. In this environment, you just can't always get the answer you need when you need it.

- **Batch Communications—*not all information is shared*.** Distributed teams rely on formal structured processes (meetings) and informal processes (e-mail) to communicate progress and assess project status. These meetings, even if they occur daily, are limited in scope and duration, forcing collaboration into a narrow timeline. That narrow timeline limits the content of the communication. E-mail, while useful, is typically brief and usually doesn't convey subtle shadings of meaning or address the larger implications of situations. The casual conversations that often take place over lunch or coffee—and that are important for collaboration on ideas—never happen, which means that you lose a critical aspect of teamwork, often without realizing it.

To close the gaps among team members, managers must conduct collaborative meetings across distances to share information, expectations, updates, and responsibilities in a timely (and therefore relevant) way. However, as I said in the chapter regarding Collaborative Execution, we're not just going to have a get-together. Effective communication and synchronization across distances— Remote Collaboration—demands a different and higher communication discipline. Since the time shifting and distance are unalterable conditions, your team must be purposeful in two dimensions: frequency and content. The collaboration process must explicitly identify what value-added information (the information that causes forward progress) must be communicated and how frequently communication must take place.

The Remote Collaboration process replicates the Basic Collaboration strategies beyond geographic or organizational boundaries so that the remote teams are fully in sync with the local teams. In short, the remote teams:

- Have a common view of the work status, issues, and work plans

- Make decisions that reflect global organizational goals

- Understand the relationships between current project status and achieving project, portfolio and organizational goals

To ensure that your team's communication is relevant, you must be clear on the *content* of your communication (what information is critical?), and focused on the *issues* (what problems need to be solved?) that will make a *real difference* (what action is needed?) to the project results.

To create meaningful collaboration, you must consider how you'll be sharing the project status or your Visual Project Board (VPB). Whatever you do—whether it's video, duplicate boards, or a software version of your VPB—it must allow all of your team members to easily contribute, distribute, and share the most important information in an orderly format that visualizes tasks, timings, and responsibilities to be completed; in short, a shared, clear vision of the project (alignment!). With access to the right information, your collaboration can be more effective. If you accommodate on-the-fly contributions and insights, your time together will encourage innovative problem solving and accountability that reinforces team action. Instead of preparing defenses, your entire team will work quickly and collaboratively to tackle problems together.

There are several elements that will dictate the frequency of your formal communication: the rate of task completion, the risk of completion behind the original schedule, and how long it takes your team to resolve issues. A one-week delay in addressing an issue may have a significant impact on the execution of your portfolio's plan.

At the beginning of a typical implementation of ViewPoint, there is a great deal of schedule risk present, and the team doesn't have a clear view of the project's status or the path forward to complete it. Therefore, daily meetings are usually required. But as the team gains control, these risks decline, and the frequency of meetings can be reduced, dictated from that point on by the length of the tasks in the project. For example, if task durations are measured in days, a weekly update is sufficient. Longer durations may call for less frequent meetings.

For Remote Collaboration to be effective, you'll need a slightly revised set of collaboration and meeting rules to foster the appropriate behaviors in all participants. As with Collaborative Execution, these meetings require a facilitator, but with Remote Collaboration, you'll need one at both ends. Ideally you should have everyone standing up in front of a board, with no muting, so side discussions don't take place. The facilitators should make an effort to foster interactions among all participants while focusing on issue identification, pressing for accountability, and addressing all other facets of Collaborative Execution.

What about Software?

Remote Collaboration requires you and your team to adhere to the same standards of visibility required for local Collaborative Execution. That means that your remote team must have a board as well. That board should be a duplicate of your local board. Do you need software to do that? Not necessarily, but it helps.

Using a visual portfolio software tool does have its advantages: You can view the board from anywhere, there is only one board to maintain, and you can automate the production of performance measurements. As an added bonus, you can keep a history for lessons learned.

For these reasons, almost everyone graduates to a software tool, but not all teams like them. Some people want the immediacy and palpability of a physical board. They like to be able to walk up to the board, pull off a card, and examine the details of each work package. In the end, it's your choice. I land on the automation side for ease of maintenance, accessibility, and performance management. Your mileage may vary!

A leading technology manufacturer found itself the victim of success: The team members couldn't meet the demand for the company's new flow meters. The problem? Each meter depended on key parts from five different sub-suppliers in different countries, which then had to be assembled and tested by two more subcontractors (also in other countries). With the suppliers spread all over the world, the team found it impossible to work toward a single goal: meeting the promised delivery deadline for the end product.

Timely communication was vital, but getting the teams to attend regular face-to-face meetings was impossible. To compensate, the project manager held tightly choreographed virtual meetings using an electronic Visual Project Board, which allowed all the team members to see the overall progress of the project and their individual roles in its successful execution. Essentially, they were able to replicate for the remote work teams the shared vision of the project status and take advantage of the collaborative execution processes they used locally.

"We feel as though we work in the same company ... and we've gotten to know our colleagues much better ... which eases communication.

"[We have] learned to put focus where it really needs to be in the project/engineering process. [We've learned to] find the constraints and focus on key resources."
— SUBCONTRACTOR'S PRODUCTION MANAGER

With real-time visibility into every link in the workflow, the team was able to detect delay risks early and take corrective actions before any problems affected delivery. As a result, productivity and delivery reliability were improved with a quintupling of capacity, a quadrupling of output, and a 23 percent reduction in lead time—which finally resulted in on-time (and in some cases, early) delivery!

If you have teams that are working remotely, bringing them into the project execution process is critical—and not just from a collaboration standpoint. Effective Remote Collaboration processes establish a foundation for further maturity in the rest of the ViewPoint processes. For you, remote teams are an extension of the local team—with the associated capabilities and capacities that must be factored into a successful project execution strategy.

When you're successful in achieving the objectives of Remote Collaboration, you'll receive all the benefits of Basic Collaboration:

- Increased employee engagement

- Improved situational awareness

- Identification and elimination of bottlenecks

- Increased productivity

- Reduced project durations

- Quick response to problems

- Increased accountability for results

- Reduced inter-functional conflict

- Improved synchronization of work and improved productivity

- Application of resources to the right tasks at the right times

- Simplification of management

- Dramatic reduction in rework

- Elimination of task overprocessing

With a shared vision of the situation, your collaboration with remote teams will be more effective. When you can accommodate on-the-fly contributions and insights, your time together will encourage innovative problem solving and accountability that reinforces team action. Instead of preparing defenses, your entire team will work quickly and collaboratively to tackle problems together and move forward.

Remote Collaboration brings the entire team of to the same level of execution maturity, so the organization can turn its attention away from fighting fires to improving the project delivery process—to further increase productivity and achieve consistent on time delivery.

Maturity in Remote Collaboration can be seen in teams that have:

- Basic Collaboration processes and behaviors successfully replicated beyond geographic or organizational boundaries;

- A common view of the work status, issues, and work plans;

- Decision-making processes in remote locations that reflect the global goals of the organization;

- Stakeholders who understand the relationship between current project status and organizational goals;

- Consistent analysis of project and task completions, issues, and escalations, which will reduce variability and improve performance; and

- Project resources that are effectively shared and managed across geographic boundaries.

CHAPTER 12

Bottleneck Management

Systematically Increasing the
Rate of Work Completion

Resources are not infinite; their availability is subject to both quantity and timing. Your project's performance is also determined by the team members' relationships to one another. A football team is no stronger than its weakest player. Similarly, a project is a chain whose strength is determined by its weakest link, its constraint. In the end, the workers at the end of the process can't do any better than those at the beginning; the worst performer in the process dictates overall project performance.

If you don't effectively manage your bottlenecks, they'll manage *you*. Your teams will be chasing the latest obstacles and reacting to problems rather than preventing them. Sometimes, those obstacles may be too large to surmount. You will simply run out of time to effectively eliminate them before they affect your project or portfolio.

Typically, identifying the bottleneck is relatively easy—the weakest link in the chain is the one that has the most work piled up in front of it (it has *much* more work than available capacity), and therefore is the one creating the most schedule risk. It's not necessarily the slowest process, but the one that has the largest load in relation to its available capacity, and thus the longest queue of waiting work. So, if you want to improve the overall speed of your project, you have to find a way to increase the productivity of that link. For example, if there are only four lanes open at the supermarket and each line has ten people in it, the market will open more lanes, and suddenly all the lines are shorter; everyone moves faster because the bottleneck has been broken. But this approach is reactionary.

It's impossible to shorten a project's duration if you don't know where the bottlenecks are.[28] Without such

---

28 In this context, I'm going to use the terms constraint and bottleneck interchangeably, even though they are technically different things. The technical name for the bottleneck is the Capacity-Constrained Resource (CCR).

knowledge—such visibility—resources are misdirected, capacity constraints are identified late, and progress is hampered by delays even as some team members stand idle. In Basic Collaboration, these bottlenecks stand out on the VPB as a group of cards queuing up at a process step, but in this level, we'll look beyond what is physically present. Bottleneck Management is not necessarily for the team member or department that has the biggest backlog of work today, but rather for the team member who is creating the most schedule risk—for today and tomorrow.

Bottleneck Management is a process used to *systematically* identify and break bottlenecks during execution. The process has two parts: identifying the future bottleneck and then breaking it. Executing is a matter of both accuracy (knowing which resource is going to be the bottleneck) and engagement (motivating people to do something about it).

Bottleneck Management entails two important activities:

- Close management of critical resources by project team

- Systematic process improvement

Finding the Future Bottleneck

The essence of the Bottleneck Management process is to continually identify those resources on the critical path that are or will be overloaded, and then resolve those overloads *before* they affect the project. The problem is that at this stage of execution maturity, teams typically do not have a very good handle on their capacity or the tasks' impact on that capacity.

Therefore, you must create a simple means of assessing resource capacity and load. Using time as a measurement of capacity is the most precise way to do this, but this typically isn't very productive; the amount of time and energy required to make a reasonable estimate isn't worth the effort. You'll spend time determining how long something takes, what's work, and what's contingency—all of which requires considerable analysis and negotiation. I'm not saying that the effort isn't worth it (see Probabilistic Planning in chapter 16), but at this stage of execution maturity, it will not pay off to the extent that it will when your organization's capability is more mature.

Rather than find a *precise* answer, get one that is *good enough*. It doesn't matter that we quantify precisely how much a resource is overloaded; all that matters is that you know it's overloaded (more than the others) and that you can make the necessary adjustments in a proactive manner, *before* it affects your project. For example, you can measure load and capacity in "stories" or "features" or "releases." Does it really matter at this point whether you are ten hours or twelve hours overloaded?

A second step in finding the future bottlenecks is choosing which resources you want to model—or even defining what a resource *is*. If you're running a software development team, I'm not sure you want to declare every developer a resource and measure their load to capacity. That's going to be a lot of work for an inadequate return. Rather, think about resource types or skills requirements. So in this case, you'd model all developers of a certain type. For example, all user interface designers could be considered a single resource (for Bottleneck Management purposes), assuming their skills are reasonably interchangeable.

You might also choose not to model resources that are easy to get. If you're in construction, you probably don't want to model laborers. But welders might be in short supply, requiring more management. In the end, choose your modeling strategy based on resource availability and commonality.

Engaging Your Team to Break the Bottleneck

We know that productivity can be improved and capacity increased by standing over someone with a whip, but that method typically only works for a little while (okay, no one does that, but we sure do drive our people hard when we're in trouble!). Your best bet to increase capacity is to change your way of working, whether it's by sequence changes, eliminating unnecessary steps, finding alternate methods, offloading work to non-constraint resources, or adding resources.

You can most easily begin to engage your team in Bottleneck Management by strengthening the principles you've already established: Collaborative Execution, Functional Alignment, Priority Control, and Control of WIP. The logic behind each of these principles—the need for visibility, collaboration, alignment, etc.—is the foundation of Bottleneck Management. As you establish the processes you'd prefer to use for Bottleneck Management, your team will be able to follow suit, understanding the motivation behind it.

Resource Flexibility

To reap the benefits of Bottleneck Management, it's not enough to simply identify and manage bottlenecks; you must consider the effect that the other resources can have on the performance of the constraining resources. This means you can't ignore the non-bottlenecks; you must actively manage the allocation of resources day to day, being flexible in putting people on the tasks that need the most attention, rather than putting more work into the system in order to keep those people busy. With a good implementation of Basic Collaboration, you're already doing this. In Bottleneck Management, we'll take this to the next level, formally building this reactionary procedure into a strategy.

From an execution standpoint, you'll be making a formal shift, going from "moving work to people" to "moving people to work." You'll essentially create policies that block work from being released merely to keep idle resources busy, and use reallocation rules instead. You'll effectively eliminate the "one resource, one project" rule.

A producer of engineered structures was having problems with schedule delays at a fabricator in China. As a result, these structures, which were part of a larger program, put the entire contract in jeopardy, and the company was facing substantial damage claims from their customer. Additionally, the fabricator was billing them for delays in delivering some components to integrate into the structure.

The analysis of the structure-build process showed that delays at the fabricator were not immediately related to the availability of these components, but would certainly affect the build schedule in a few months. So they dispatched a small team to increase the supply capacity of the most critical bottleneck component.

The component was planned for production in Malaysia, so that's where they went. Initially, the team was focused on improving productivity at the supplier, but the rough-cut capacity analysis of their critical resources showed they had a bigger problem. Despite all the work they had done to increase short-term capacity, they still wouldn't be able to produce on the required timeline, especially since that facility had competing demands from other projects. Further complicating the supply situation was the relative immaturity of the plant's execution processes, which meant that the supply was unsteady, thus diminishing hopes that they would get better.

The team looked all over the world for other suppliers, evaluating their bottleneck capacity, and eventually they found a few. They didn't find a lot; industry capacity was tight, and they found just enough with a small margin for error. They outsourced some of that production to those other suppliers, and based on their demonstrated capacity, sent additional components their way.

Simultaneously, within the production process, the same critical operation was the constraint at each production location. Each of these suppliers was very closely monitored to ensure that they could deliver. They engaged the local teams to carefully manage the constraint, taking action to ensure that its capacity was exploited, and that other resources were able to support the plan. This additional capacity broke the bottleneck for the entire project, and the component never delayed fabrication.

Effective Bottleneck Management will further reduce your project duration and significantly reduce project schedule risk, and you'll get a boost in your delivery reliability and productivity. Another implication of achieving this level of maturity is that your role as a project manager includes process improvement. After all, how can you reduce project duration if you don't possess the basics of process improvement?

Maturity in Bottleneck Management can be seen in teams that:

- Look across all projects to roughly determine the workload for critical resources;

- Present the workload and resource availability to stakeholders for action;

- Are flexible in allocation of resources, moving resources *to* the work, rather than moving the work to the resources; and

- Engage both management and resource teams to break bottlenecks before they affect schedules.

When bottlenecks are managed, projects proceed more quickly and smoothly, without delays caused by unplanned resource shortages. The project team facilitates ongoing process improvement, bettering performance for *all* projects in the portfolio.

CHAPTER 13

Delivery Promising

Making Realistic Delivery Commitments

Clients and customers always want to know in advance: When can they expect to receive their deliverables? Providing an accurate answer, though, is only possible if your understanding of the entire system's capacity—the resources you have available to address the volume of tasks at hand—is up to par. At the Improved Coordination level of maturity, no detailed task-level plans have been made, and resource pools are undefined. The loop between planning and execution is still not fully closed.

Meanwhile, your customers still need a date. The project team needs a reliable way to promise and follow through with deliveries. When your team has mastered managing the bottlenecks, schedule risk, and dates, then you can provide a reasonably accurate delivery date.

Typically, dates are promised with greater regard for market requirements than for process capability and resource availability. Too often, work gets launched into the system because the customer wants it right away, and the organization, being responsive, wants to do the best they can. The additional work throws the entire system into chaos (remember Little's law, discussed in chapter 10). Not only do you undo all the good work you've done in Basic Collaboration, but you also set unrealistic expectations for your customers and management, creating the opportunity for unpleasant budget and schedule surprises down the road.

Delivery Promising prevents this chaos. It's the process of evaluating the impact on your portfolio of new work and projects. Delivery Promising ensures that prior to the introduction of this work, there is ample consideration of resource availability and existing work. It prevents overconfidence in promising delivery dates, ensuring that new work can be accepted without negatively impacting other projects in the portfolio. The objective of Delivery Promising is to offer your clients or stakeholders realistic predictions of completion dates for milestones or project deliveries. Using the Delivery

Promising process, you can insert a piece of work into the process, and it will meld with the other work while allowing your in-progress projects to be completed on time. You'll accept as much work as is feasible without disrupting the system, and you will still deliver reliably.

The key to understanding the importance of Delivery Promising is to think back to the sections covering the control of WIP (chapter 10). Delivery Promising builds on these foundational principles by planning to stagger the execution of projects at the rate at which the system (constraint) can handle it. This may mean delaying the start of the project, but when the project is released, it can proceed quickly and smoothly.

We know that the key process characteristic that determines project lead time is the available capacity at the bottleneck resource. We also know the critical path for the project. You and your team can make a reasonable prediction for project delivery based on just these two elements. You won't be checking for resource conflicts across the entire project, but only at the critical resources, which, for these purposes, will be "good enough." How far you go in your development of this process—and what is "good enough"—will depend on the complexity of your projects and your tolerance for risk.

In Bottleneck Management, you have already created a rough-cut capacity-load profile for all of your critical resources, and you know the constraint of the system. Recall that the performance of the entire system is determined by its constraint, so this is the critical piece of information to consider first. The opportunity to introduce new work into the system emerges when that load declines.

With Collaborative Execution, you've already made some good estimates of the critical path, so you know the approximate duration of most projects. In order to determine the delivery date, you can make a very good estimation of the completion dates of *all* projects by staggering the new project into the existing process. Figure 3 below shows three different projects staggered on the bottleneck resource in dark shading.

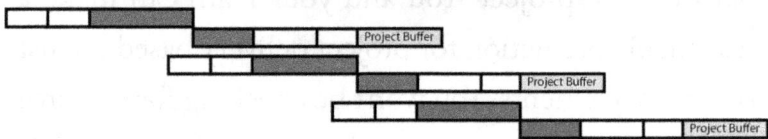

Figure 3

The Delivery Promising process is more than just staggering dates; it also considers the realities of the marketplace: client emergencies, opportunities, and demanding customers. What if a customer needs their deliverable faster than anticipated, or they want something where there is a resource conflict? An important part of the process is the escalation and reconciliation process with which, when there is a conflict between availability and customer demand, management can make rational decisions about how to proceed. Sometimes you might want to call another customer and request a delivery delay on another project. Sometimes you might realize that you can't delay any of your pending projects or tasks, and so you'll need to spend money on more resources or consider an alternate supplier. Each of these decisions has different implications for different parts of the organization. The escalation and reconciliation process allows for effective governance in that it pushes decisions to the right level of authority and accountability.

Delivery Promising is an important step in managing the future of your projects. Doing it well will have a positive impact on your customer relationships and improve delivery reliability. Your management team will also be happier, you'll see a reduction in the spending required to recover your schedule, and resource productivity will rise. In short, more projects, in less time, on time.

An organization with maturity in Delivery Promising has:

- A clear policy stating that project on-time delivery and actual project lead times are *always* used to determine normal project completion dates;

- Project duration estimates that reflect the impact of shared resources;

- Managers who take into account the impact of new projects on the entire portfolio before committing to delivery dates; and

- A willingness to take portfolio-wide actions when due dates are threatened.

If you don't promise new work and delivery dates properly, you'll set your team up to fail and set your customers up for disappointment. By mastering Delivery Promising, you increase your probability of delivering on time—and on budget.

Chapter 14

Schedule Risk Management

Preempt Problems to Deliver on Time

No matter how good your plan may be, managing schedule risk is essential to project success. Risk will always be present; the question is, is it effectively managed? In organizations with immature execution behaviors, risk manifests itself as surprises that derail workflows and delay completions. Unless a means of early identification and mitigation of risk is available and utilized, your team is always going to be reacting. As a result, your projects are doomed to delays, constant firefighting, and rising costs. Getting your team out in front of risk is the goal of Schedule Risk Management.

Traditionally, project managers have tried to reduce schedule risk by projecting completion times for projects based on the sum of individual task completions in the critical path. But these task-completion time estimates are suspect. When managers ask for time estimates, teams and individuals add "contingency" time that allows for uncertainty and anticipates setbacks. Contingency time in itself is relatively benign—in fact, the need for contingency time is essential—but when added up, the time collectively added by various teams and individuals makes the project much longer than it needs to be, clouding the actual schedule risk and adding unnecessary delays to project completion.

Worse, management has lost control of the project to the degree that resources determine their own contingency time buffers. The project team as a whole loses clear sight of the project; they cannot distinguish between the work and the contingency. The management team then must either react conservatively to keep everything on track (forcing unnecessary overtime and expediting), or wait until the situation is clarified. Waiting sets the team up for a late reaction, which delays delivery even more.

Additional risk is created when an organization fails to consider the needs and timing of the *multiple* projects it has going on. Even if contingency time is considered, the subject matter experts who will be executing the plan are rarely consulted during schedule development—and the result is unrealistic task durations and a plan that is all but impossible to execute.

Too often, the "horse is out of the barn"; the project can't be stopped midway to correct problems that should have been anticipated during the project planning process. During execution, the problem becomes one of focus. If your project plan is broken, how can your team know which is the most significant risk to respond to at *this* moment? Successful project managers must maintain constant situational awareness relative to overall project schedule performance, identifying the work remaining versus the time remaining—*before* time runs out.

Schedule Risk Management is a statistical method for maintaining that situational awareness and improving a project manager's ability to manage and control work and resource priorities. This in turn enables management to direct action early enough to prevent late deliveries. When applied across a portfolio of projects, Schedule Risk Management aids project and resource-level decision making to accelerate the completion of *all* of the projects that share resources. It improves project team decision making by identifying the project tasks with the highest schedule risk throughout the life of the project. Teams can then act early to ensure project completion on or before a committed project or milestone delivery date.

In order to effectively manage schedule risk, project teams must separate task work time from task contingency time. Since most task duration estimates are pessimistic and allow for plenty of contingency time, the team must shift the planning from the worst-case scenario and identify the most likely time to complete the work and save the contingency time for the overall project. The sum of all the contingency times therefore establishes a time buffer that protects the project completion date(s). In this section, I'll cover the elements of Schedule Risk Management: **Estimating Task Duration, Progress Reporting**, and **Schedule Risk Ratio.**

Uncertain Task Durations Mean the Project Must Own Contingency

Let's start with the most basic assumption about projects: that they are full of uncertainty. There's uncertainty about the deliverables themselves, especially if there is technical risk (i.e., new things being created), and there's uncertainty about the work that will be necessary to achieve those deliverables, since many projects are "one-off" affairs.

Therefore, you should realize that the tasks and their durations within the project schedule are an estimate, a forecast. Those who provide these estimates usually have a limited understanding of the work to be accomplished, and they may be pessimistic in their estimations. Few people are trained in estimating task duration, so for most projects, the tasks that make up the project plan are not accurate, making the project completion date(s) suspect as well. In short, duration estimates in most projects are not to be trusted.

To correct this deficiency, we could focus on the most obvious problem and strive for more accurate estimates. However, this will take a long time! Here's a more workable solution: Rather than decompose the duration estimates to make them more accurate (even though that would be helpful to our projects), let's consider only one element—the contingency time. We can assume the remainder of the estimate is the work.

The contingency time is the amount of time we have in the schedule to compensate for risk. We often call this the time buffer, or just "the buffer." This time is not owned by individuals or functions, but rather by the *project*. The reason for that is to protect the integrity of the purpose of contingency—reliable *project* delivery dates as opposed to individual *task* completion dates.

Thus, since the project is full of uncertainty, the project itself must own and manage the buffer.

As the project progresses, you should expect that task duration variation will occur, both favorable and unfavorable. In some cases, they will cancel each other out. However, you should expect that the buffer will be consumed as work is accomplished; you'll have more in the beginning and less at the end. In a perfect world, you would have zero on the day you deliver your finished project.

Knowing the amount of time remaining to do the remaining amount of work is valuable for the organization; it tells you where to focus your attention. This knowledge is a simple, straightforward tool to govern portfolio risk.

Report Progress as Time to Completion to Reinforce the Right Behavior

From a progress-reporting standpoint, consider the primary question that customers and management really want answered: "Will my project be on time?" For your project team, this is essentially a risk management question. It's one that traditional critical path-based methodologies cannot adequately answer,[29] but it

---

29 Many project managers use float to assess project delivery risk, using a Critical Path Method project plan.

can be answered in an unexpected way. We can inform stakeholders of both the status of the project (as determined by the percentage of critical path completed) and the risk that it will not be completed on time (as a percentage of project buffer consumed).

Specific milestone and task completion dates are often used to report project and milestone statuses. There are legitimate reasons for using specific, deterministic dates in the day-to-day progress-reporting scheme, but since there is so much uncertainty in the project, neither your project teams nor your customers benefit much from such reports. When deterministic dates are absolutely required, I prefer to use floating milestones (with associated dates) to update the management information systems when just these dates need to be tracked. This approach can accommodate contractual milestones (fixed dates), which are managed using the Delivery Date Management methodology (discussed in the next section). Passing the expected completion dates and final completion dates to an enterprise project management system can drive the billing and supply-chain management systems. In any event, you shouldn't be worried about task completion dates way out in the future, but you certainly should manage the dates that are important to the portfolio, the organization, and your customers.

Let's keep in mind that the purpose of individual task reporting is to enable you to get a read on your current position. While it is nice to know that a task is 20 or 30 percent complete, "percentage complete" doesn't answer the question of when the task will be finished. For example, you may have completed 97 percent of a two-week task, but if the final component of that task is expected in one week, reporting 97 percent progress does not convey the fact that you have 50 percent of the estimated duration remaining. Reporting percentage complete distorts the true status of the project and often can hide a significant delay.

We should instead ask our team members to consider only the task at hand and report the time remaining until completion, which is much more useful (and more reliable) information. This request will encourage your people to work on task completion with an emphasis on speed, and enable you and your management team to spot potential delays with greater accuracy. It also prevents Parkinson's law[30] from coming into play and delaying task completion even more.

This kind of progress reporting enables you to line up behavior with the goal of the project (remember

---

30 Work expands so as to fill the time available for its completion.

Functional Alignment from our first level of maturity?). It also allows you to identify and capitalize on early task completions, allowing the project to regain buffer time. Driving progress reporting toward time to completion instead of percentage complete will encourage team members to work on one task at a time (no multitasking!), and thereby accelerate progress.

The Schedule Risk Ratio:
Your Early Warning Indicator

The Schedule Risk Ratio is a tool that allows you to accurately identify small problems before they become truly major problems. Even early in the project, you can determine whether you're ahead or behind schedule by identifying how much risk you have, adding another dimension to your Priority Control processes.

The ratio is determined by how much buffer remains compared to how much work remains along the critical path, and assigning that buffer to the oldest in-work task along that path. Assessing a ratio for each task provides a normalized set of priorities across the project and the portfolio, thereby reducing multitasking.

Use the Schedule Risk Ratio to Direct Project Activity

Using a simple green-yellow-red system, you can easily communicate project status and activity to the team and to the rest of the stakeholders. When the percentage of buffer remaining is more than the percentage of work remaining on the critical path, your project is in the "green (we're on track) zone." Your project is in the "yellow (caution) zone" if your percentage of buffer remaining is less than the percentage of critical path work completed. When the ratio of work remaining significantly exceeds the remaining buffer—say, 70 percent

Project 1 has the higher priority (for resources, help) because it is using buffer faster than it is making progress

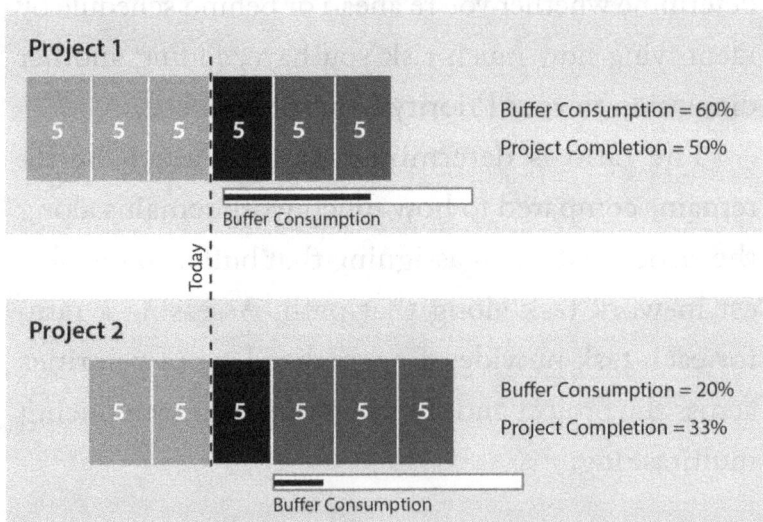

Project 1

| 5 | 5 | 5 | 5 | 5 | 5 |

Buffer Consumption

Buffer Consumption = 60%
Project Completion = 50%

Today

Project 2

| 5 | 5 | 5 | 5 | 5 | 5 |

Buffer Consumption

Buffer Consumption = 20%
Project Completion = 33%

of your work remaining and only 30 percent of your buffer—you are probably in the "red (do something!) zone" of project execution.

Now, don't wait until the project goes "red" before you do something. When the ratio is in the yellow zone, develop a buffer recovery action plan to respond in case the buffer consumption trend continues and your project goes red. If it does, your project team's buffer recovery plan should go into effect.

With this plan, you will likely be focused on reducing the duration of the longest task on the critical path. Any specific tactic—process changes, additional resources, offloading—is good as long as the project deliverables aren't compromised. Just don't assume you'll work your way out! Don't jump to rescheduling your entire project, either; your recovery plan absolutely must get done before the project due date is modified.

Use the Risk Ratio to Set Task Priorities

The Risk Ratio is assigned to the open, in-work task in the critical path. When there are multiple ongoing tasks, a Risk Ratio is assigned to each one. Utilizing the Risk Ratio provides your team with a normalized priority system that can function as an early warning tool across a portfolio of projects. It brings the Priority Control process to greater maturity. This enables you to be more strategic in resource allocation and directing activity, and to allocate resources more effectively. If you can see that one project in the portfolio is behind, you can borrow resources from another project that has more buffer for support.

As your team manages the project buffers, you will be monitoring not only the open tasks, but the upcoming ones as well, reinforcing the "future orientation" you established in Basic Collaboration.

Black task in Project 1 has the higher priority because it has a lower Schedule Risk Ratio

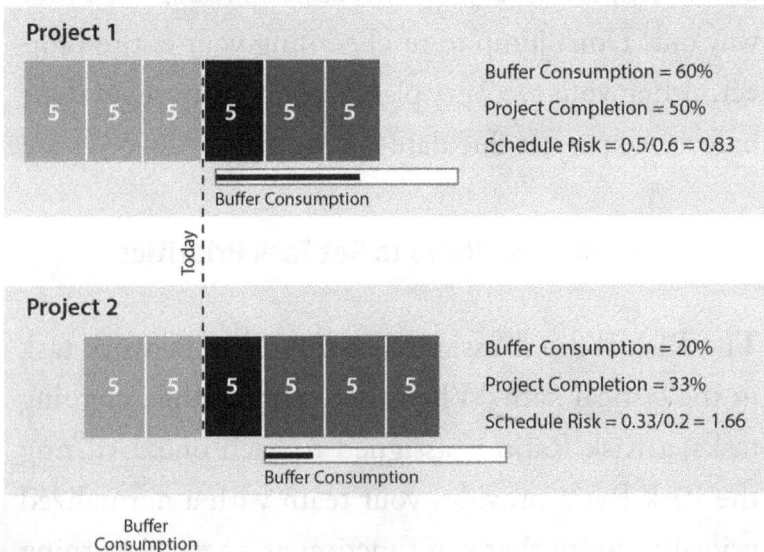

Project 1

| 5 | 5 | 5 | 5 | 5 | 5 |

Buffer Consumption = 60%
Project Completion = 50%
Schedule Risk = 0.5/0.6 = 0.83

Buffer Consumption

Today

Project 2

| 5 | 5 | 5 | 5 | 5 | 5 |

Buffer Consumption = 20%
Project Completion = 33%
Schedule Risk = 0.33/0.2 = 1.66

Buffer Consumption

Buffer Consumption

Making Realistic Risk Assessments
with Remote Teams

When your teams are distant from each other, it's difficult to get an accurate view of the work to be done; all your teams have a fixed delivery date, but the path to that date is obscured because the component tasks are often not well understood, nor are they appropriately aligned to the project's goals. Dispersed teams are then forced to make educated guesses about the remaining work of the other team(s) and their schedule realism. The real risks to delivery remain obscure.

Additionally, different teams may have different ideas and assumptions about contingency and work, further obscuring the picture. During execution, there are often different standards for what is or should be reported, preventing the team from understanding the overall project risk.

This is why, when you have remote teams, the Remote Collaboration process must precede Schedule Risk Management. For all projects, especially when there are remote teams, the buffer is centrally managed.

To master schedule risk, distributed teams need to:

- Develop a shared understanding of the work and the safety;

- Report the remaining time durations of individual tasks; and

- Measure work remaining versus buffer remaining.

Essentially, your distributed teams must use the same processes that you and your local team use to make task duration estimates and report progress. Remote teams don't get their own buffer; they are part of the same project, and so they share the same project buffer.

For the United States Air Force during Operation Desert Storm, urgency was defined by the most extreme condition possible: American forces waiting on the ground for new weapons systems. Three Air Force project managers oversaw one new eagerly anticipated "smart weapon" project each. All three project managers, working from different locations, were overwhelmed by the pressure to meet wartime demands, and it seemed that they needed additional resources to meet their deadlines.

In the end, the project team took a different tack. Instead of adding resources, they linked the three projects and created a project portfolio with one resource pool, clearly defined tasks, clearly visible project buffers, and a distinct separation between the work and the contingency. Project plans were based on lengthy but possible task durations. The safety pulled out of the tasks was aggregated into buffers that protected key project deliverables and each integration point along the critical chain of tasks to the final deliverables.

At the beginning of the process, each manager's vision was limited to his own project because of the lack of visibility between locations. With the appropriate collaboration methodology in place, however, workflow management was put on an objective footing. Each project manager was able to see and understand the total work in the system and the risk associated with the entire portfolio.

To get an accurate picture of project progress, consistency was required not only in the workflow management, but in the team's behavior as well. To that end, team members changed the way they reported the work. Where they originally were reporting what percentage of the task was complete, they now communicated how many days they would need to complete their assigned activities. This eliminated uncertainty for the critical tasks and clearly showed where the schedule risks were.

In this new and improved environment, overall portfolio priorities were determined by expectations from the war zone, and project buffers were based on the true need. This, in turn, drove the local task priorities. The project work remaining and the amount of buffer remaining served as a measure of risk, allowing each project activity to be objectively prioritized. As a result, all three projects were successfully completed on time—and none were completed at the expense of the others.

The Schedule Risk Ratio provides a measure of the health of the project schedule, tells your team which tasks it should focus on and which ones need additional attention, and alerts the team when they must take action to ensure project delivery by the committed date(s).

Armed with advance knowledge, you can act early and strategically, adjusting priorities and resource assignments to ensure timely delivery. You'll have greater control, better decision-making ability, and shorter project durations.

You'll know that your organization effectively manages schedule risk when:

- The work duration for tasks on the critical path is clearly separated from the contingency duration;

- Variability in task duration is accounted for, using time buffers at the project level;

- The project time buffer is explicitly managed; and

- Schedule risks are normalized across the project or portfolio, and the level of risk is used to prioritize resource assignment and activity.

When schedule risk is effectively managed, your projects are more likely to meet deadlines without allocating extra budget dollars to overtime or expediting efforts, or using additional people.

CHAPTER 15

Delivery Date Management

Maintaining Delivery Date Integrity
Across the IT Systems

Engineering Procurement and Construction (EPC) and complex engineering organizations rely on information systems to plan, manage, and synchronize various aspects of projects—most frequently, the intricacies of obtaining necessary components and sequencing activity.

However, priority management is often overlooked in information systems, and the main drivers of execution priority are often ignored: contract milestones and delivery dates. There is an abundance of them, and the more intricate the project and the more sophisticated the information system, the more dates there are to manage. As one of the inputs to determine Schedule

Risk, we cannot overlook the importance of the accuracy of the date to set the execution teams down the path to successful completion.

While the accuracy of the dates is important, it is equally important to manage them during execution and to understand the implications for the project if one of these dates is changed. Do the right people know about it? What are the implications for the various parts of the project? How will their project priorities be affected? Who is responsible for keeping date information updated and accurate? Who will communicate these changes? How will they do it?

The Delivery Date Management process answers these questions and protects the integrity of the priority system by ensuring that all dates used to drive the priority system are correct and synchronized.

When I talk about "Delivery Date Management," I mean the administrative aspect of managing dates in the system. We know from our earlier section that management of schedule risk depends on valid date information—if you don't have good date information, your entire system of priorities will break down. I've found it helpful to have one function (or person) whose sole responsibility is to manage the dates in the system.

Working with Milestone Dates

Milestone/integration dates for large projects are often set far in advance. Once your contractual dates are solidified, other levels or functions of the organization often add more dates and milestones to manage, and they protect their individual pieces of the project schedule. These well-intentioned actions inadvertently create execution problems for your organization as a whole—there's no alignment within the entire team. Too many intermediate (and usually unimportant) dates lead to issues like date confusion, priority confusion, and the effects of Parkinson's law.

In complex projects, different levels of management and function often obscure important dates. Teams strive to protect their own delivery commitments, obscuring the true requirements of the project and the customer, distorting priorities, and causing other teams to work on the wrong tasks. Some work is completed early and gets stuck in the workflow, while the work necessary to maintain schedule progress is completed late. Obscuring the true delivery requirement causes disagreement on the core priorities of the organization, wasting management attention on tactical issues and stealing focus from potentially more important strategies to drive the projects and portfolio forward.

That's not to say that dates are unnecessary. In many environments, there are tasks associated with dates that must be managed: contract compliance dates, supplier delivery dates, payment dates, and so on. The problem is that there are too many *unnecessary* dates. Apart from the problem of managing the volumes of dates, most project management methods do not address the risk created when you add more complexity. Have as few dates as possible, not only because they can increase the duration of the project, but also because they reduce your flexibility and ability to respond to variation during project execution. That being said, if the project process requires specific milestone dates, these must be buffered and managed as smaller subprojects within the context of the portfolio of the larger project.

The Impact of Date Changes

The key to successful Delivery Date Management is ensuring that all of the IT systems in the organization have full and accurate critical date information, whether it's your milestone dates or dates that customers set. In order to do that, it's crucial that you maintain visibility, and that you have a process that ensures that those dates are lined up in the various information systems (including the manual ones!).

You may have to do a little detective work to see how the dates are (or are not!) connected. Don't automatically assume that when the delivery date goes into the contract form it flows all the way down to the supplier. There are multiple dates floating around in the system—the contract itself, sales orders, supplier deliveries, the schedule plan (which is not necessarily what drives the supply chain), e-mail correspondence, verbal promises, etc. Sometimes the connection is manual, and it only gets done at the beginning of the project. There are likely to be time offsets (contingencies) at different levels of the project and different segments. The people responsible for managing at these different levels will be hard to pin down. The foundation of the Delivery Date Management process is understanding the relationship between the systems, so spend some time here.

Dates do change for myriad reasons. Customers' needs change. Dates are renegotiated as you or the customers learn more about the project. Delays happen. If you're building a tunnel in northern China during the winter and one of the mountain passes is closed because of snowfall, it's no one's fault that supplies can't get there at the projected time—but the adjustment still needs to be made to compensate for that delay.

Date changes must be treated with the same diligence as a full-scope change, because date changes *are* a scope change. To many people, a date is just a number in a computer somewhere, and they don't realize the true impact of changing it. Changing a critical date, though, affects the complexion of the entire project. You cannot manage schedule risk without careful attention. Dates are the driver of activity within your project, and if there's a delay, suddenly priorities must be re-sorted, and your people will need to work on different tasks. If the dates aren't right, you'll have the wrong people working on the wrong things at the wrong time, and you won't get the expected results.

In managing your delivery dates, think about the following: Who is the person who monitors them? How will he or she do it? How can you ensure that there are no conflicts? A process to manage a date change is akin to the process you use in Delivery Promising: You'll want to go through the evaluation and potentially the escalation process. It doesn't matter what the information system is. All that matters is what is in it and who controls it. At the other end, for example, if a supplier's delivery date changes, it has to be put into the system so that the priorities change appropriately, activities dependent on that supplier can be accomplished, and progress can continue.

Delivery Date Management protects the integrity of your schedule risk ratio, and thus your early warning system and priority management system. When your data has integrity, you'll further reduce priority shifting, which in turn will reduce task switching and multitasking, leading to increased productivity with naturally reduced costs. The management process will be easier, too. The clarity of work priorities will reduce task synchronization errors, leading to increased productivity, shorter project durations, and less rework.

You'll know that you and your team are effectively managing delivery dates when:

- Project and milestone delivery dates are the sole (or at least primary) drivers of project and task priority;

- There are processes and procedures in place to ensure delivery date integrity;

- Dates are accurate expressions of customer expectations and/or organizational commitments; and

- Dates in internal IT systems for master documents—e.g., sales orders WBSs, etc.—are accurate and aligned.

In order to support and deliver on changes in customer requirements, the dates that drive priorities have to be consistently managed, with synchronization between internal information systems and external demands. Without a single priority driver in the organization, other priority systems crop up, destroying all the good work you've done so far.

Improved Coordination Summary
Objective: Deliver on Time

ELEMENT	BEHAVIORS	RESULT
Remote Collaboration	• Basic Collaboration processes and behaviors successfully replicated beyond geographic or organizational boundaries • A common view of the work status, issues, and work plans • Decision-making processes in remote locations that reflect the global goals of the organization • Stakeholders understand the relationships between current project status and organizational goals • Consistent analysis of project and task completions, issues, and escalations, which will reduce variability and improve performance • Project resources effectively shared and managed across geographic boundaries	For work accomplished at remote or distributed teams, all the benefits of Basic Collaboration: • Increased employee engagement • Improved situational awareness • Identification and elimination of bottlenecks • Increased productivity • Reduced project durations • Quick response to problems • Increased accountability for results • Reduced inter-functional conflict • Improved synchronization of work • Application of resources to the right tasks at the right times • Simplification of management • Considerable reduction in rework • Elimination of task overprocessing

ELEMENT	BEHAVIORS	RESULT
Bottleneck Management	• Looks across all projects to roughly determine the workload for resources • Presents the workload and critical resource availability to stakeholders for action • Is flexible in allocation of resources, moving resources to the work rather than moving the work to the resources • Engages management and resource teams to break bottlenecks before they impact schedules	• Further increase in productivity • Reduction of project durations • Improved delivery reliability • Increased productivity
Delivery Promising	• A clear policy that states project on-time delivery and actual project lead times are always used to determine normal project completions • Project duration estimates that reflect the impact of shared resources • Managers who take into account the impact of new projects on the entire portfolio before committing to delivery dates • Portfolio-wide actions taken when due dates are threatened	• Improved delivery reliability • Reduced expediting costs • Increased productivity

ELEMENT	BEHAVIORS	RESULT
Schedule Risk Management	• The work duration for tasks on the critical path is clearly separated from the contingency duration • Variability in task duration is accounted for, using time buffers at the project level • The project time buffer is explicitly managed • Schedule risks are normalized across the project or portfolio, and the level of risk is used to prioritize resource assignment and activity	Early action on schedule risk Further increase in productivity Improved delivery reliability Reduction of multi-tasking, resulting in increased productivity
Delivery Date Management	• Project and milestone delivery dates are the sole priority drivers • There are processes and procedures in place to ensure delivery date integrity • Dates are accurate expressions of customer expectations and/or organizational commitments • Dates in internal IT systems for master documents, i.e., sales orders and WBS's, are accurate and aligned	• Reduced priority shifting, leading to reduced multitasking and increased productivity • Reduced task synchronization errors, leading to increased task completion velocity, shorter project durations, and improved productivity

By achieving maturity in Improved Coordination, you and your team will have successfully bridged the gap between Basic Collaboration and the highest level of maturity, Integrated Planning and Execution. Having already achieved Basic Collaboration, you will have successfully spread those principles throughout your organization, and begun to delve into more complex project management principles and practices. Your remote teams will be aligned with your local teams. Your prioritization skills will be honed, and your attention to detail will now be directed to the *most important* details. Your on-time delivery performance will have improved significantly, and you'll get there without mad dashes to the finish line or stress on your team. Productivity will have further increased, and project lead times will have shrunk even further.

Particularly important to this stage is perfecting both Bottleneck Management and Schedule Risk Management. These processes will feed directly into your understanding and implementation of Integrated Planning and Execution. With the foundation of Basic Collaboration already laid, you will see performance improvement in all of your ongoing projects, and your organization will be well on its way to world-class delivery!

Stage Three:
INTEGRATED PLANNING AND EXECUTION

Managing Risk and Optimizing Performance

Having made it this far in execution maturity, you've gone far beyond your competitors. You're feeling like you're on top of your projects, but there are still too many surprises—surprises that could be avoided if you expended more effort thinking about the future. You still haven't solved the resource-sharing problem of having idle resources in one part of the portfolio and shortages in others. If you're working with suppliers and subcontractors, you probably have limited visibility into schedule risk until it's too late. You've probably got some sort of risk management process in place, but it's not integrated into your execution process—you have plans, but they're rarely updated until there's a problem. You can *taste* the opportunity for more reductions in cost and budget, which will drive your delivery advantage beyond any competitor's reach.

The final and most mature stage of the Project Execution Maturity Model is Integrated Planning and Execution. This level of maturity is where we can firmly and formally close the loop between best-practice planning and execution. Earlier I discussed how planning isn't the solution, and I differentiated between planning for control and planning for execution. In this phase, we'll reconcile the plans for control with the plans for execution, and we'll do so by moving from accomplishing tasks to consistently achieving milestones for projects that generate profits. We'll establish a constant cycle wherein the plan leads to execution, and the current activity and execution informs the plan's updates. The plan will constantly be updated to reflect new information and understanding that each step in the execution process provides.

This level of project execution maturity is focused on three processes:

- **Probabilistic Planning,** which refines the processes that manage uncertainty in the project by integrating risk management with planning and execution

- **Capacity Management,** which improves productivity by developing a coherent capacity strategy aligned with project and portfolio objectives

- **Subcontractor Integration**, which
  focuses on reducing subcontractor and
  supplier-related uncertainty by managing
  and aligning the critical aspects of their
  performance with the objectives of the
  project, portfolio, and enterprise

We began in Basic Collaboration with managing projects and portfolios at the task level, but we're now looking at management over the course of the next one, two, or even five years. At this level, you'll become more strategic in your view and activities, integrating all the elements of project planning and management to optimize performance over the long term. You'll also be able to make the best use of your resources across projects, portfolios, and geographies.

The objective of the Integrated Planning and Execution level is to elevate the risk management capability of the organization by rapidly integrating the feedback from execution into the project plans. It addresses three kinds of risk: task duration, resource availability, and supplier and subcontractor delivery.

Integrated Planning and Execution applies Probabilistic Planning principles to the schedule and provides new information for decision making, allowing for early risk mitigation and execution strategy development. Furthermore, it improves the ability to identify resource shortages and conflicts, which in turn improves and reduces delays in execution across the entire portfolio. It also reduces delays from suppliers and subcontractors by applying risk management tactics to sourcing strategies. Then, during execution, it integrates the supplier with the overall program, portfolio, or project.

When you have progressed to this level of execution maturity, your improved execution behaviors will already have rewarded you with increased productivity, increased rates of on-time delivery, and reduced project durations. The next series of improvements moves from the medium-term tactical to the longer-term strategic, from managing projects to managing *enterprises*. At the highest levels, successful organizations embrace execution methods and apply lessons learned throughout the entire organization. Managers will spend most of their time managing the future—planning for and managing risks and resources, and developing process capabilities for competitive advantage. Achievement of this level of maturity will deliver *ongoing* reduction of project lead times and costs, and consistent, superior delivery reliability.

As these areas of the highest level of maturity are greatest in sophistication, I must abbreviate my explanations of how to achieve them. I will provide an overview and the basic principles, but the practices to put all of them into effect must be part of another book—maybe even three of them!

CHAPTER 16

Probabilistic Planning

*Using Variation and Risk
to Improve Project Performance*

So far, we've been dealing with very simplistic planning and execution processes and activities, working with simplified workflows and major deliverables. Now that your execution teams are humming, you're ready to step up to the next level and expand into greater details and get the benefits that proper planning can deliver. I've said before that planning is not the leverage point in your project, but I've also been careful to say that planning is not unimportant. Now that the foundation for execution is in place, your team is ready to engage with a well-built project plan.

By "well-built," I mean a plan that's built for execution; a plan that *can* be executed. These are not the same kinds of plans you have been building; those plans are for control. Plans for execution are distinctly different from plans for control. Planning for control is what we've been doing for the last fifty years: driving down to the details, identifying the tasks to accomplish and the resources that will complete them, time phasing them, etc. These complex and comprehensive plans are based on a premise of control: *"Comparing actual results with desired results and deciding whether to revise objectives or methods of execution."*[31]

This is most people's idea of control. They watch what happens, compare the events to what was expected, then change things to bring reality into line with their expectations. If too many things fail to match their picture of reality, even if that picture is only in their heads, they must add more detail to the plan. In this way, they can watch all the details (we have software) and make adjustments when things go awry.

I propose a different definition of control: *"A reactive mechanism to handle uncertainty by monitoring information that can point to a threatening situation, and preparing*

---

31 Fogarty, Blackstone, and Hoffmann, Production and Inventory Management, 1991.

corrective actions accordingly. [32] In other words, Control is a process in which we watch for areas of increasing risk, and then respond before the actual risk event. In essence, we build the plan with the assumption that things will go wrong (remember Murphy's law from chapter 4?), even if we don't know precisely *what* will go wrong.

All the minutiae, the various connections, and the sheer volume of items involved in projects—and by extension, portfolios—exceed any single manager's span of control. These details may be important to someone, and they should be. When managers have all that detail, though, it imposes additional management complexity and volume on the execution team. Therefore, our plan(s) must be tailored to our span of control. Those plans will then be used to respond to risks, and will drive behavior during execution.

No plans are 100 percent guaranteed to ensure completion of a project by a particular date. Probabilistic Planning strives to *maximize the likelihood* of completion at that date. By using Probabilistic Planning, you'll be able to make a quantitative prediction of a range of project outcomes based on the likelihood of risk occurrence and effect. Rather than providing fixed dates (as in

---

32 Schragenheim, *Run the Business—A Computer Simulation* Workshop, 1999.

deterministic planning), you'll be able to create a range of dates with corresponding likelihoods of achievement. For example, if a customer wants to know when first oil will be delivered (i.e., when the oil first arrives from a new well), your calculations will tell you, "There is a 50 percent chance of achieving first oil by date X or sooner, and a 90 percent chance of achieving it by date Y or sooner."[33]

Of course, this isn't what you would tell the customer. Instead, your customer should receive a committed date based on your organization's tolerance for uncertainty and risk, which is all stated during the planning process. For some customers, you may feel that 75 percent is adequate; for others, even a 90 percent certainty may be scary depending on contractual penalties or damages. To be clear, the risk of delivery is stated during the planning phase of the project. In order to raise the likelihood of executing to 100 percent, your project team must aggressively manage the buffer during execution, which I discussed in the chapter on schedule risk (chapter 12) and will address later in this chapter.

The fundamental difference between traditional project planning and Probabilistic Planning is the emphasis on identifying and managing uncertainty

---

33 Probabilistic Planning is not just for dates. It can also be applied to establish a probable range of project costs and returns.

during execution—in essence, the implementation of Control as I have defined it. Probabilistic Planning uses statistical methods to quantify and manage uncertainty and schedule risk. It starts with understanding the inherent variability in project task durations (also discussed in chapter 12). I framed this as the unreliability of task duration estimates, but even the same task performed over and over will not have the exact same duration every time.

Probabilistic Planning also quantifies the impact of risk events on delivery schedules—which improves management decision making to control those risks—and thus on the overall financial viability of the project and the portfolio itself.

From a practical standpoint, Probabilistic Planning will help you identify the critical issues sooner than deterministic methods do, meaning that you and your team can implement early intervention and prevention strategies to deliver on time. It may involve the use of Monte Carlo simulation techniques. Concrete statistical information drives the forecast of likely task and project durations. Your resource contention and shortages are identified and resolved. Time buffers are subsequently incorporated into the project plan to absorb unfavorable task-duration variation.

A Practical Approach to Risk Management

Entire books could be (and have been) written on risk management, and you no doubt have extensive experience with the subject. My intent in this chapter is not to provide even a rudimentary explanation of risk management, but rather to clarify the process, and how risk management and a probabilistic approach contribute to achieving this highest level of maturity.

Recall that earlier I discussed the idea of contingency in task estimates, and the need to separate that from the planned duration of a task. That contingency is for risk, isn't it? In the Schedule Risk Management process, we've moved from the premise that variation and risk are best managed at the task and resource level to the premise that they are best managed at the project level.

Some think that the best way to approach variation and risk is to drive them out of the process. This is a worthy goal, but an impossible one, unless you can find a way around the laws of physics. Since all risk cannot be removed from reality, a better, more practical approach to managing it is to find ways to contain its effects. Using a probabilistic approach, you can find a range of potential outcomes and build alternatives and execution strategies around those. The approach you take to both planning and execution, then, is dependent on your perception, analysis, and tolerance of risk.

In life, the risk we mitigate is dependent on our perception of the *consequences* of a risk event. In other words, our planning and execution responses are calibrated to our judgment of the outcome. If, for example, you have a very important meeting scheduled at the office for 1:00 p.m., and you know that it typically takes you half an hour to get there from your house, what time do you consider leaving? Would you leave at 12:30, or would you give it a little extra time just to be safe? If you leave your house at 12:00 or 12:15 (allowing more than a half hour), you've made a decision that accounts for the risk effect of late arrival. If you have only a typical meeting with a colleague at 1:00, though, chances are your decision will be different; you're more likely to leave at 12:20 or 12:25. Either way, you've made a decision about risk—about the impact of an uncertain event affecting your objectives.

This perception of risk (both actual risk and how we interpret its implications) influences your decision making, and when you're working on big projects, that risk is magnified. If you have $40 million at stake as opposed to $200, what would be the repercussions of finishing late or missing a critical deliverable? That's not to say that risk management is solely a function of the potential financial impact of the decision. Each person (and organization) has a different threshold for managing risk; some will tolerate more than others. Your tolerance will have a significant influence on your efforts.

Building the Probabilistic Plan

The first step in the Probabilistic Planning process is to build the probabilistic planning and execution strategy. In figure 4, below, I refer to it as building the baseline network. In the context of Probabilistic Planning, "network" refers to the technical relationships and durations of tasks and resources.

Probabilistic Project Management: Schedule Project

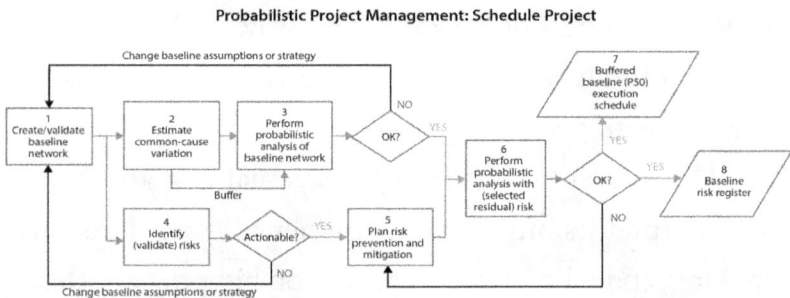

Figure 4
Probabilistic Planning Process Overview

Figure 4 shows the process of creating the probabilistic plan. Note that it addresses the two causes of variation I called attention to earlier: *common* and *special*. As we discussed in chapter 12, common-cause variation is the variation inherent in the system, while special-cause variation has some definite cause—e.g., an identified project risk. Common-cause variation is the reason you'll see variation in task durations when you perform the same task on five different projects. You will manage special-cause variation using your risk management process. The reason for the distinction is that "the type of action required to reduce special causes of variation is totally different from the action required to reduce variation and faults from the system itself."[34] Buffers (and management of buffers) are the tools to manage common-cause variation, and to identify when action is required to control special-cause variation (beyond those items identified in the risk management process).

When we think about the process of Probabilistic Planning, what we're doing is combining the task duration variation concepts (also introduced in chapter 12) and the standard risk management process in a detailed, integrated fashion. In Probabilistic Planning, we have

---

34 Deming, W. Edwards, *Out of the Crisis*, Massachusetts Inst. Technology, 1982.

three basic input activities (respectively corresponding to boxes 1, 5, and 6 in figure 4):

1. Create or validate baseline network

2. Plan risk prevention and mitigation

3. Perform probabilistic analysis with selected residual risk

These inputs lead to two outputs (boxes 7 and 8 in figure 4):

- Buffered baseline (P50) execution schedule

- Baseline risk register

Planning for Execution

The foundation for an effective probabilistic schedule is a high-quality unconstrained, deterministic schedule that includes a good Work Breakdown Structure (WBS), milestones, planning assumptions, and good work package (task) duration estimates, which results in a validated project network.

The objective of the first step is to validate task durations and task relationships, and to ensure that the planned durations are actually those that are most likely. Only when this has been achieved can we conduct a probabilistic analysis.

In chapter 12, I wrote about task estimation. At that level of execution maturity, you're focused on the tasks on the critical path. At this level, we're now applying these principles to the entire project in order to build a comprehensive plan for execution. There are two aspects of this: the technical aspects and the consistency across the portfolio.

Let's deal with the latter first. In our experience at Pinnacle Strategies, we've found that when managers and organizations build schedules, there often isn't a lot of consistency in how plans are built. Maintaining consistency across the portfolio, as always, requires accountability. So who owns this process? How does it get taught? Even organizations that have a "standard process" will find inconsistency among plans that are built using their "standard" process.

Many organizations that have well-defined processes fail to use them across the portfolio. For example, using CTR (cost-time-resource) documents that support the WBS. The CTRs describe the contents of the project in detail: What are we doing? What will we deliver? What resources are required to produce these deliverables? What's the timeframe? What is the cost estimate?

A CTR can—and *should*—be created for every significant level of the project. If you're building a garage, you'll have a CTR for the roof. You'll create a different one for the flooring. You'll draw up yet another CTR for the electrical work and another for the framing. CTRs are necessary for resource loading (consumption), but are rarely created with enough detail to support this activity. Without CTRs, it is quite difficult to build a valid project plan. Yet, we find that this critical element of project planning is rarely done consistently, and that the outcome for valid plans is predictably poor.

Another example of planning inconsistency lies in the difference between the plan and reality. Most plans are created with the assumption that the project will begin at the earliest possible start, but in practice, project managers often use a latest possible start. Additionally, there's still a lot of preference (what we typically do or want to do) built into project plans, and plans aren't necessarily based on the technical requirements. There's typically no process to challenge these preferences, and no identification of a true best practice.

Now, let's take a look at the technical aspects of planning. There need not be a conflict between planning for

control and planning for execution, but there is a certain
level of detail required to build a schedule that will be
useful during execution. The Ten Commandments for
Network Building address the tasks necessary to create
a plan that works.

Ten Commandments for Network Building

1. **The networks will represent what *will* be
   done, not what *should* be done.**
   The schedule must reflect reality. A
   schedule is not an aspiration; it's the best
   statement of what you think you will be
   doing. It reflects your strategy and your
   tactics.

2. **The network is constructed to answer a
   question or questions by the organization.
   This question dictates the scope and detail
   of the network.**
   Typically the question is, "When will the
   project be completed?" Different questions
   asked by people with different spans of
   control generate different networks, but
   many planners create a single network that
   tries to answer *all* of the questions. One

all-inclusive network isn't workable; more effective is a series of plans that are related to each other and that answer the different questions and needs of each function or phase within the project.

3. **Each task in the network produces a tangible deliverable.**
Each task or node in the network produces a tangible deliverable (or deliverables) or output, and becomes an input for the next link (task) in the chain.

4. **The network describes the tangible deliverables of the project.**
Every task that is in the project plan produces a deliverable so that the project network is a description of the series of deliverables to be produced. In other words, the deliverables are made clear.

5. **Tasks are completed by resources that require concrete deliverable inputs (reports containing information, machines, components, etc.).**
By requiring a tangible input, each task has a corresponding person accountable

for its completion. The person accountable (a manager, for example) may not be the person doing the actual work.

6. **Task predecessor relationships are determined using sufficiency and necessity logic.**
   In sufficiency and necessity logic, we are differentiating the elements that are *sufficient* to complete a task from those that are *necessary*. Necessary elements are individual elements required. If you are building a fire, wood would be a necessary element. Sufficient to a task is the group of necessary elements that can make a task happen—in other words, wood is a necessary element to building a fire, but it's not the only necessary element. The technical requirements of each task, necessary and sufficient, are the sole determinant of the order in which tasks happen—not what we'd *like* to do.

7. **Task durations are estimated using aggressive but possible (most likely probability) durations.**

We do not build extra contingency into the tasks. Contingency (buffer) belongs to the project.

8. **Project milestones and intermediate objectives are few, and are fixed in time and buffered ONLY when the entire project's success depends on it (i.e., the customer demands it).**
   This rule is akin to the principle of managing risk—dates, just like risk, are only set and managed at the project level.

9. **Risk events and potential tasks will be identified as such.**
   Make your risk activities explicit. Include risk in your plan so that you and your team are prepared. This may result in multiple plan scenarios, which is a reasonable and expected outcome.

10. **The network must have the buy-in of the entire project team before it is considered complete.**
    Everyone involved—including resources *and* project managers—needs to be part of the planning process. If they don't buy in, how can it be considered realistic?

Following the commandments of network building will result in a statement of the requirements, deliverables, resources, and handoffs to deliver your project. Now it's time to consider special cause risk.

Risk Planning

Most projects don't require a sophisticated, in-depth risk-planning process, but each project demands at least a basic level of risk management. The bigger the project, the more complex the risk-planning process needs to be; you might consider team-based workshops that complement a web-based risk registration and management system. For smaller projects, risk planning can be as simple as a desktop exercise with a spreadsheet. Simply put, the level of risk planning should be determined by the amount of resources and tasks required to get the job done; the more moving parts a project has, the more risk it will have.

In order to apply the appropriate degree of risk planning, it's crucial that you focus on those tasks that are most critical to reducing your schedule duration (the longest or highest risk tasks on the critical path). Don't overthink this; having a few good responses to the most significant risks is a far more supportive tactic than making a detailed list of every possible problem that might come up, because as we already know, you simply cannot plan for every contingency.

What's the most likely duration of the task? What potential variation is there? What are the conditions that would result in task durations of 10 percent probability, and what are the conditions necessary for 90 percent? In other words, what would have to happen for the task to take the shortest amount of time, and conversely, the longest duration? You won't assess every single task (again, you can't plan for every contingency; don't expend your time and energy in trying), but you will assess the most significant ones along the critical chain.[35]

Resource estimation, too, is a critical part of your risk planning. It's easy to build a project and assume the resources will be there. For the most part, the resources are likely to be available, but the chief complaint among project managers is that there aren't enough resources. Resource availability must be recognized as a significant part of the planning process and of the project itself, but we don't necessarily do all the things required to support an effective resource plan.

Estimate the need for resources in the same way

---

35 The longest sequence of dependent tasks considering resource availability—sometimes called the resource-leveled critical path.

you would calculate other probabilities. At this level of maturity, there will be some variation in what resources are available, when they're available, and the quality of them. Probabilistic Planning for resources can cut bottlenecks off before they cause problems.

Lessons Learned in Planning

Probabilistic Planning Improves
the Quality of the Plan

Creation of a probabilistic schedule provides an effective quality check of your deterministic schedule. This alternative way of viewing and analyzing the schedule leads to many improvements in the schedule, task definition, and logic.

The probabilistic analysis process identifies unexpected impacts of constraints—bottlenecks—and lags in the deterministic schedule. Scheduling best practices should minimize or eliminate these constraints in the plan. If they must remain, ensure that they are visible. One of the objectives of building the baseline schedule is to eliminate any preference constraints to provide a technically-based plan as the standard to which all others will be compared.

Probabilistic Planning Must Integrate with Risk Management Processes

The definition of any particular risk is often misunderstood. The risks as stated in the risk register must be understandable to all project stakeholders, with the consideration that personnel assignments often change during the life of a project. It must include a specific format for stating risks, probabilistic information, and the basis for the quantitative risk estimates. In our experience, we have found a number of instances in which no one currently working on a project understood what a given risk statement in the register meant.

Probabilistic Planning Must Use Existing Project Management Best Practices

Another problem we've witnessed is that many projects don't effectively use a single Work Breakdown Structure (WBS) to integrate project work, meaning there's nothing for a schedule to relate to. This complicates understanding how to link risks and actions to tasks, as task identifiers change with schedule modifications. In addition, it complicates the integration of the functional systems for schedule and action tracking relative to the project system.

Executing the Probabilistic Plan:
Buffer Management

We introduced basic Buffer Management in chapter 12 with the concept of Schedule Risk Management. With Probabilistic Planning, we take the implementation further. To apply Buffer Management to the formal plan, we can incorporate it into the larger planning process and integrate the schedule risk ratio across all tasks and work streams, beyond the critical chain and into feeding and parallel chains.

Buffer Management increases risk visibility, improving project and resource-level decisions to accelerate the completion of all the projects and reduce their duration. It also achieves better resource utilization by enabling team members to focus on project tasks and prioritize them according to schedule risk. In turn, this enables the team to complete all tasks sooner, as we've eliminated a major source of multitasking. Buffer Management also improves project team focus by identifying early on those project tasks that require action in order to ensure timely project completion. It enables managers to commit to high probability fixed dates while using the variation information (which is provided by Probabilistic Planning) to guide execution activity.

Using the probabilistic schedule analysis, you've placed time buffers at the ends of those project task chains, leading to a desired project outcome date (e.g., first oil). Buffer Management then uses the schedule risk ratio and your response rules (which you have already set in lower levels of execution maturity) to control execution of the project. Buffer Management provides normalized task priority information across the entire portfolio. It tells your project team which tasks or projects need focused attention, and when the team must take action to ensure project delivery to the committed milestone.

Probabilistic Project Management – Executing Projects

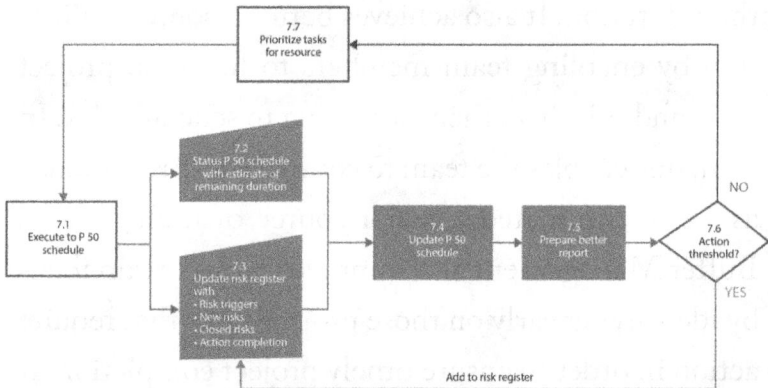

Figure 5

Buffer Management execution ensures that the project team focuses on the right tasks to complete the project on or ahead of schedule.

Risk Management Process During Execution

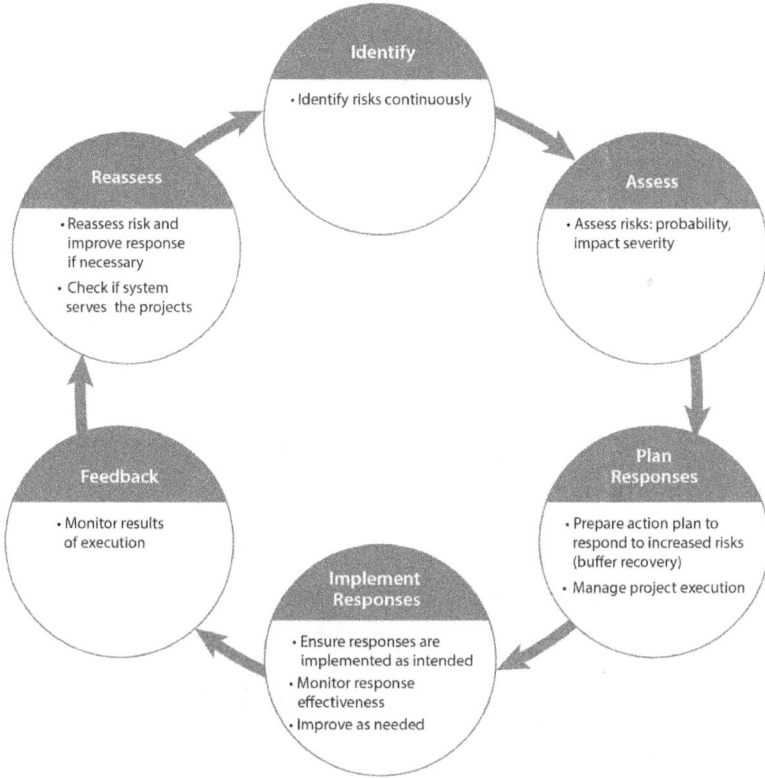

Identify
- Identify risks continuously

Reassess
- Reassess risk and improve response if necessary
- Check if system serves the projects

Assess
- Assess risks: probability, impact severity

Feedback
- Monitor results of execution

Plan Responses
- Prepare action plan to respond to increased risks (buffer recovery)
- Manage project execution

Implement Responses
- Ensure responses are implemented as intended
- Monitor response effectiveness
- Improve as needed

Lessons Learned in Execution

- **Traceability from the risk register to the probabilistic schedule is necessary to relate any variation to the risk cause.** Project work package leaders (WPLs) working on multiple projects with a plethora of tracking mechanisms, like schedules and action lists, may have a hard time focusing on what risk needs to be addressed in what order. Each functional organization typically has their own work management system for both project tasks and action items. These systems often do not tie directly to the project management systems. Thus, extensive manual effort is often required to synchronize these tools across all projects. There must be a common tool set that meets the needs for governance and execution.

- **There must be a clear definition of task completion.**
  Some WPLs determine task completion dates by the availability of people to schedule a review meeting—i.e., they work to schedule a meeting with a reviewer, and the date of that reviewer's availability determines the completion date for the task. This approach wastes project time and ultimately delays project completion, as the WPLs cannot complete sooner than those dates. It significantly reduces the potential gains of probabilistic scheduling/ Buffer Management. This is typically resolved in Basic Collaboration, but now that there are more tasks, additional definition is often needed.

A Dutch company with more than 6,000 employees worldwide, SBM Offshore is a leading provider of floating platform production and mooring systems for offshore oil and gas industries. SBM's Atlantia division was charged with fulfilling a warranty cable replacement project for one of its clients. Under the most stable conditions, replacing undersea cables is a complicated process. But after initial planning had begun, changing requirements significantly increased the project's complexity. With just one week's notice, the installation date moved up a full month, *and* the number of cables to be replaced increased from four to nine.

SOLUTION: Coordinate preparation and installation management plans that allow for flexibility.
The team approached the project in two steps: Probabilistic Planning processes for installation preparation *and* for managing the installation itself. Given uncertainty about the availability of the necessary diving vessel and about the condition of the cables themselves, careful prep work was considered essential—and

subsequent events demonstrated the wisdom of this prudence. It took three versions of the installation plan to arrive at one that was technically feasible. Then the diving vessel became available prematurely, moving the planned installation date up by a month. Once onsite at sea, the project team discovered that nine, not four, cables had to be replaced. Because SBM's client did not allow work at night, the project team couldn't complete the work in its planned twenty-four-hour timeframe and had to make an additional trip. Further, people moved on and off the project at a moment's notice, requiring rapid one-on-one training to coordinate new arrivals with revised plans.

RESULTS: 27 percent reduction in project duration.

Despite the obstacles, SBM successfully completed more than twice as many cable replacements as had been expected to be necessary in remarkably less time. The preparation phase was completed five weeks earlier than planned, and the installation phase was finished nine days earlier than expected—even after the project had been moved up a month!

Probabilistic Planning allows organizations to make better decisions based on the perception of acceptable risk. The probabilistic scheduling process improves the credibility of the project plan by:

- Providing a greater understanding of the work to be accomplished through:

) Consistent task estimates across groups

) Reliable task relationship linkages

) Greater assurance of risk and team focus

- Improving control during execution through:

) Earlier identification of problem areas

) More proactive problem resolution

You can expect additional benefits from probabilistic scheduling and Buffer Management during execution, including:

- Increased availability of resources, which will effectively deliver more projects;

- Improved visibility of project risks and their impact on schedules;

- Greater flexibility to respond to risks; and

- Improved on-time completion of projects.

These benefits will come as a result of better planning and better deployment of people to project tasks, which will in turn reduce waste and inefficiency in task performance. If we can help team members to focus on one project task at a time and pass on their result to the next task in a timely fashion, then we can reduce delays and rework.

You'll know that your organization is correctly utilizing Probabilistic Planning when:

- Project plans account for variability, risk, or ineffective behaviors;

- The critical chain is explicitly identified and managed;

- Task duration estimates are treated as forecasts rather than commitments;

- Schedule-risk time buffers are clearly stated and managed;

- Execution is based on deliverables to be produced; and

- Monte-Carlo or other probabilistic analysis methods are employed to evaluate risk.

CHAPTER 17

Capacity Management

*Preventing Resource Shortages
from Blocking Project Performance*

People's assumptions about what resources are available—
and when—often prove false, especially when projects
share multiple resource pools. Without a consistent
approach to managing capacity, work will be assigned
and released under misconceptions about availability,
overloading some resources with multiple projects and
creating unplanned delays while others are underuti-
lized. If you fail to effectively manage long-term capacity, you risk undoing all that great work you did in stage
one of controlling WIP, recreating an environment con-
ducive to multitasking, and losing all the gains you've
made in productivity and speed.

"Capacity" can be defined in a variety of ways, not just by the amount hours of a particular machine or skillset available. In some environments, "capacity" is synonymous with infrastructure availability. For example, the sleeping capacity on offshore oilrigs determines how many people can work simultaneously. That in turn, determines the rate of asset improvement.

The need for a structured Capacity Management process is even more pronounced in organizations that have resources distributed across different geographic regions. Organizations often have different competencies in different locations (which you will have begun to address in stage two), and those competencies don't necessarily match the work required or the deliverables to be produced in the timeframe in which they must be done.

Capacity Management is a management process by which the executive/leadership team achieves focus, alignment, and synchronization among all functions in the portfolio. The process includes updating resource requirements from all projects in the portfolio, which leads to a resource-loaded execution plan and a resulting financial plan. The process frequency and planning horizon depend on the specifics of the portfolio. Short project cycles and high variation require more frequent updates than long projects with little variation.

With Capacity Management, you will be looking several months (or even years) into the future. You'll be reconciling expected demand on critical resources adjusted for the probability of start dates and the likelihood that potential projects will be given the go-ahead with your resource supply. The resulting signals are provided to both sourcing (for equipment or material resources) and human resources (for critical skills). Based on lead times for acquisition of these critical resources, Capacity Management will trigger the acquisition or hiring process. If temporary demand spikes in critical resources are expected, or if there is significant uncertainty, decisions may be made to outsource rather than permanently acquiring the resources.

A properly implemented Capacity Management process routinely reviews portfolio resource demand and supply resources and "replans" quantitatively across an agreed-upon rolling horizon. The replanning process focuses on changes from the previously agreed-upon portfolio plan. While Capacity Management will help you to understand how the organization achieved its current level of performance, its primary focus is on future actions and anticipated results.

Capacity Management utilizes the probabilistic plans that you've already created for resources and anticipated projects, and assesses the resource requirements across the entire portfolio. The process works to solve the problem of not having the right resources in the right place at the right time, which reduces the need to react to bottlenecks and thus reduces overall resource costs. Up to this point in our execution maturity, we've been doing very rough planning, dealing with what we have already. At this level, we will plan more strategically, forecasting demand and making plans to acquire resources we don't yet have.

Capacity Management resolves an important conflict: How can you ensure that you have enough resources without spending too much money? If you buy too much, then profitability is damaged. If you don't buy enough, profitability is damaged in a different way; you won't be able to produce what you've sold, and you either have to hire more resources or get more expensive ones—whatever it takes to satisfy the market and your stockholders.

In order to adequately manage capacity, you'll need to have a process in which:

- The projects and their tasks are mapped to your resources;

- You've identified the conflicts between what the plans require and what you actually have; and

- You can respond appropriately.

When capacity is managed effectively, all project and portfolio managers will use a single standard resource model to plan and execute their projects. Resourcing, resource estimates, and resource utilization numbers will be consistently derived and reported across all projects and used to allocate resources sufficiently across the portfolio. Resource capacity, load, utilization, task performance, and task completions are tracked, and the metrics of past performance are assessed regularly by team leaders to determine hiring needs, project capacities, and any training requirements.

Considering Constraints

In manufacturing, managers typically consider a forecast of capacity requirements and of availability (sales and operations planning), and then reconcile the two to achieve the objectives of their business. Capacity Management is quite similar to this sort of reconciliation—but there's also an additional aspect wherein *constraints* must be considered. Consideration doesn't mean just *finding* the constraints; it also means *choosing* them. In paying attention to your constraints, you manage the pacing (of schedule progress) resource for your portfolio. Once you've chosen that pacing resource, the goal will be to fully utilize it. In order to accomplish that, you must have enough protective capacity in the other non-constraint resources—extra capacity that will not be explicitly allocated to a project or task.

This idea—that one or a few resources will be fully allocated and the rest will be *under* allocated—may be difficult to sell, but the physics are undeniable. If all resources are fully utilized, there can be no sprint capacity, and no capability to recover from unfavorable variation. The more sprint capacity you have, the faster you can recover. However, too much capacity increases the cost of your projects, so you can't have too much. Capacity Management strives to strike a balance between too much protective capacity (at most resources) and too little. At the end of the day, the additional expense of carrying some "extra" capacity is often negligible when you compare it to the impact of being late.

At this level of maturity, we know that the constraints and bottlenecks will always exist, and we know how to identify and break them. If we can identify them, we can choose them. Rather than merely reacting to the situation at hand, we are actually changing our reality, planning exactly where our bottleneck will be.

Choosing the constraint also makes the task of focusing during execution easier. It also allows you to directly influence an important aspect of your portfolio performance—its return on investment.

Bearing these factors in mind, it makes sense to choose a resource that is difficult to acquire, difficult to outsource, and therefore typically expensive. For example, you may choose the engineering group to be the constraint of your projects because skilled engineers are much more expensive and scarce than, say, welders or painters.

If your company specializes in projects or products that require high levels of technical ability or involve intellectual property, you probably don't want to outsource that work, because if you do, then that capability is out in the marketplace for your competitors to use. I once worked with a microchip company that didn't own any manufacturing equipment at all; their entire business was built around their design. They chose their software development group as their constraint, and used resources outside the company to manufacture their products. Their business, then, was centered on the most expensive, specialized resource that no one else had, and as a result, they were able to maximize their capital return.

What about the Other Resources?

Following the choice of a primary constraint, you must then ensure that you have enough of that resource to support successful execution of the portfolio. At the same time, we cannot lose sight of the other resources involved, because of course they're needed too. In managing the non-constraints, you must keep them from becoming bottlenecks so that your chosen constraint can be fully utilized, and simultaneously ensure that there is enough capacity both to feed enough work to keep the constraint working and to accept the volume of work it produces.

The good news is this: Because you've done a good job selecting your constraint resources, these other resources won't be the most expensive or difficult to procure. It may mean you need to have extra resources on hand; because of process variation, you cannot fully exploit more than one or two resources in a portfolio at a time, so sprint capacity is necessary in order to catch up on an as-needed basis. Additionally, you must consider the probabilistic schedules and their impact on capacity requirement forecasts. You'll have a probable (most likely) amount of load on most of your resources. That probable amount will affect both the volume and the timing of the load (since we know that tasks have uncertain start and finish times). Protective capacity compensates for both.

In a way, having this protective, extra capacity is akin to having a volunteer fire department on hand at all times. In execution, though, this capacity will be absorbed through task duration variation. We know that Murphy lives—and this is the most practical way of coping with Murphy's law.

Reconciliation: Strategic Portfolio Planning

Your portfolio has multiple projects—ongoing and prospective—with different organizational value. Reconciliation includes both the full decision-making process—in which projects are given priority based on business value—and how the process is put into action.

A common (portfolio-wide) approach to planning and execution is necessary to reconciliation, which you will have established in Probabilistic Planning. You will primarily be utilizing:

- A standard approach to creating plans— the foundation of Probabilistic Planning, covered in chapter 16; and

- Shared resource pools—using a common approach to identify and manage the capability and availability of all resources.

Reconciliation is a management activity that not only responds to consideration of your choice of constraint, but also aligns that consideration with the entire portfolio. It's a business planning process, not just a capacity planning process. You'll be making decisions about which projects will have the priority on scarce resources, and which resources should be acquired and when. And you'll be choosing where to allocate resources based on your judgment of which projects bring the most business value.

As with the rest of the principles at this level of maturity, you'll be working on the future. You'll assess the risk of each prospective project and the probability of winning the bid, and you'll balance that risk against the risk involved with the acquisition of resources.

At its foundation, reconciliation is about managing the supply and demand of resources. It's a delicate balancing act. You begin with a prioritization process, making judgments on the sequence of these projects, which projects should stay in the portfolio, and which ones you want to plan capacity for. (Because, as we know, we can't plan for everything.)

Having prioritized your projects, you will then go back to the resources, first assessing the impact of each project on the constraint. You'll have to stagger or pipeline the projects according to the constraint's capability. This process requires you to avoid overloading the non-constraints so that they can continue to support the constrained resource you've already chosen. If you have all the capacity you need, then there's no action to be taken—but that's seldom the case. In most scenarios, there are more projects than capacity.

Even though you are working to control the impact of supply and demand, the "demand" is never certain. Projects get cancelled or postponed; circumstances change. Work that into your reconciliation process. If the price of oil has dropped significantly and your project's value corresponds to that price, the overall portfolio would benefit from pushing that project back until the situation becomes more certain, as you can then direct your resources to more lucrative projects. But this is just a simple example of economic considerations in the trade-off. The point is that change is the only constant in your portfolio. Recognize it in your process. In this way, you not only consider the constraint, but also *protect* it, translating your resource capacity management strategy into a competitive advantage.

I don't want to end this section without mentioning that the accuracy of plans for future or potential project demand, which you use to identify long-term capacity requirements, does not need to be as high as for the projects you are currently executing. The predictions are the "best guess" of what you have *today*, and they will guide you in making resource acquisition decisions. As the project draws closer, the requirement for precision increases. Most of the time, you can use templates based on past work to get close enough for the granularity of your required decisions for future work.

In turn, choosing your constraint makes your deliveries more predictable and provides a clear link back to your demand requirements, since it's easier to evaluate the impact of new work.

A division of a Fortune 500 company needed to coordinate engineering efforts at the portfolio level to meet global demand. But at the operations level, where common components were frequently custom designed to meet higher-level program requirements, chronic miscalculations in timing and capacity management continually threatened the integrity of the entire system, exposing the organization to penalty payments. To address the issue, they created a new business unit to apply component-level engineering discipline to design and build standard components that could fit in a variety of configurations. But with no visibility into projected demand, no recorded history of supply-chain capacity, and a staff composed almost entirely of new engineers unfamiliar with previous projects, the new unit was launching in the dark.

When our team arrived at the new unit, our client was in the midst of a dramatic shift in fulfillment strategy, from engineer-to-order to configure-to-order, in which common elements could be produced in *anticipation* of likely demand. While the new strategy promised improvements in on-time delivery performance and shorter lead times, it required the one thing the business did not have: visibility based not just on open orders, but on current bids and future forecasts modeled on prior history. In an environment in which qualified suppliers are few—and those available have very limited capacity—this lack of visibility meant a loss of control over critical elements of the supply chain.

Subsequent investigation identified the root problem: the business unit had no process to match planned demand to planned capacity. Because of this gap at the front end of the process, the business unit and its customers were squeezed at the back end, forced into expensive scrambles for components. The team addressed the problem with a capacity planning process that included the following elements:

Demand Planning: To close the gap between project initiation and parts processing, they developed a Planning Bill of Materials, a placeholder for the formal Bill of Materials that was created at the systems launch and would allow the business unit to forecast demand. Once combined with the open orders, component demand moved from virtual invisibility to a rolling three-year global forecast of component-level demand by the product family and SKU.

Supply Planning: With a reliable forecast demand in place, they needed to assign capacity, matching demand to both internal and external sources. They then consulted with key suppliers, creating "resource profiles" that accurately reflected capacity by examining potential constraints, influences on throughput, shift schedules, and available man-hours. These resource profiles identified both the planned capacity and the maximum capacity potential of available sources; with a new rough-cut capacity planning tool, the company could synchronize supply and demand, and weigh reasonable alternatives should capacity fall short.

Sales and Operations Alignment: After establishing supply and demand planning procedures, the company needed the ability to adjust capacity decisions as much as twelve months in advance of projected challenges. The team implemented monthly Capacity Management planning meetings among senior management to review status changes, ensure supply and demand alignment, monitor the business units' performance, and drive decisions on any issues that could put customer deliveries at risk.

In just a few months, they transformed the components operations from a liability that worked in the dark to a productive unit that could forecast its demands as much as three years in advance. Aligning supply and demand enabled them to optimize their critical resources and move from reactive to proactive management. In their monthly Capacity Management planning meetings, they regularly reviewed capacity, resolved supply problems, and aligned all functions to a single operating plan integrated with a global strategic plan. The rigor of the process gave them the control that they sorely needed while simultaneously improving customer service, cost, and resource utilization.

Capacity Management, in short, is about the reconciliation process. It is about choosing the constraint, and making sure that we have enough capacity at *non*-constraints in order to fully utilize that constraint resource. Effective project and portfolio management requires an accurate understanding of resource availability, and it requires visibility into current and future workloads. It also requires the manager to make informed decisions based not only on anticipated project loads, but also on the fluctuating needs of the entire organization.

Your organization will reflect effective Capacity Management when:

- There is one standard model for assessing capacity across the organization;

- Management has visibility into both the resources present and the resources needed;

- Reserve capacity is available—there are not just time buffers, but *resource* buffers; and

- Resources that are scarce or difficult to obtain are managed well (not wasted).

CHAPTER 18

Subcontractor Integration

Reducing Supply-Chain Risk

Subcontractors and suppliers are often a critical part of successful project execution. Aside from the pressure to manage a significant part of the project budget, understanding schedule risk from subcontractors and suppliers has always been nearly impossible. There is seldom any reliable method for project managers to see into the supply chain, except the reports from the procurement staff, who have hundreds (if not thousands) of items to look after.

For most suppliers that produce a deliverable on a specific day, it's impossible for the project manager to get a read on delivery status until either the item appears or it doesn't. For subcontractors, having on-site managers and frequent reporting diminishes the risk somewhat, but there are still obstacles that prevent transparency between the partners.

For a project team that has reached this level of execution maturity, working with suppliers and subcontractors is a bit frustrating; they seldom have anything more than base-level execution process maturity. A big part of Subcontractor Integration, therefore, is applying the Project Execution Maturity Model to their organization. You'd think that this would be a fairly straightforward task, but "improving" an organization you don't have direct control over presents some unique challenges. The biggest challenge is trust.

The main issue to get around in working with suppliers and subcontractors is that they're paid to deliver a specific component on a specific date. With large projects that span longer periods of time, these suppliers are typically paid progress payments—the timing of which is usually determined by the suppliers themselves—and they are not necessarily aligned with the needs of the overall project or portfolio. For example, many projects pay subcontractors based on earned value. However, more value earned isn't the same as more schedule progress. Suppliers and subcontractors can work on tasks off of the critical path and still earn value; they get paid even if they do not advance the project toward on-time completion. They get paid even if they deliver late. Earned Value is a great way to lie to your stakeholders.[36]

As I discussed in chapter 8 (the section that covers Functional Alignment), bringing everyone together to share the same goal (completing the project quickly) is critical to ensuring that the execution process is transparent and speedy. That's pretty easy to do when everyone works for the same company (well, eas*ier*), but suppliers and subcontractors have one objective, and it's the same as that of every other business: to make money for *their* business. Suppliers' and subcontractors' behavior, then, is going to be geared toward profits for their organization and not necessarily your portfolio. Subcontractor Integration resolves any conflict over progress and payment between the two organizations, aligning them throughout execution to make *your* projects move forward quickly.

Effective Subcontractor Integration encourages productive execution behaviors to these external parts of the workflow, aligning the interests of the subcontractors with those of the company. For subcontractors, this is achieved in two ways: one, by providing visibility into

---

36 Yates, *How to Lie with Earned Value,* 2005.

the suppliers' workflow to enable early identification of problems, and two, working with them to synchronize their work with that of the project. To manage risk from suppliers, this is achieved with supplier selection strategies and by using time buffers (as you would for any other task or deliverable).

In Subcontractor Integration, there's no direct management of other people's businesses. What you can do, though, is assess and manage the supplier's delivery and schedule risk. How might you do that? *By using the Project Execution Maturity Model.* You can ask the same questions of a supplier that you've asked of your own company: Is there Functional Alignment? Priority Control? Control of WIP? Collaborative Execution? What about the processes from stages two or three? Are they present? By using the model for your own purposes, you can present a best practice for the way they manage their delivery.

The activities necessary to achieve this level of maturity are:

- Separating suppliers from subcontractors

- Sourcing and selection

- Alignment of project objectives

- Delivery Risk Management

) Integration of lead times into planning activities

) Managing inventories for long lead items

- Execution Performance Management

) Collaborative Execution

) Remote Collaboration

) Subcontractor Capacity Planning

Not every supplier or subcontractor will be a candidate for this process—only those with the highest schedule risk. Note that levels of risk will change throughout the project. You may implement Subcontractor Integration with one or two suppliers right from the beginning of the project, until the risk is eliminated. You might then move from supplier to supplier during the life of the project as supplier risks increase during execution. In either case, your Subcontractor Integration process should be light on overhead and heavy on schedule impact. You should spend no more than 3 percent of your total contract value on this process. That's pretty cheap insurance!

A Subcontractor or a Supplier?

Different kinds of suppliers require different risk management strategies. The difference between a supplier and subcontractor is the difference between an organization that provides specific deliverables and one that provides multiple deliverables. It's the difference between buying a refrigerator and hiring a kitchen-remodeling contractor. Both will affect the delivery success of your new kitchen, but one involves the purchase of a generic item from a company that produces millions of the same item, and the other involves the purchase of a service to produce a custom deliverable (or multiple deliverables). One is loosely managed, and one is more carefully managed.

For your project, you're probably not going to try to manage the manufacturer of your refrigerator, but what if it's a custom unit, made to suit your specific needs? How do you assess the delivery risk? What can you do to mitigate that risk? On the other side of the coin, there's the contractor. You'll be seeing them almost every day. They'll get plenty of attention, and your risk mitigation strategy will be quite different. So it is in Subcontractor Integration. Your primary effort will be focused on your subcontractors, but you can't ignore your suppliers.

Delivery Reliability in Sourcing and Selection

The supplier risk mitigation strategies are quite simple and straightforward. What's different in ViewPoint is how we think about these strategies and where we apply them.

Let's begin with picking the lowest risk supplier. Usually, the procurement people make this decision for the project team. Rarely is delivery risk considered in the sourcing decision, much less balancing this risk against the cost of late project delivery. So the project team is nearly always using the "least cost" provider, and "cost of being late" is not considered.

Having the least-cost supplier is not *always* going to have an effect on project delivery—unless, of course, they're late and that deliverable is on the critical chain. If that's the case, what to do?

The time buffers are your primary source of protection against supplier delivery risk, so you'll be protected—to a point. Your Buffer Management execution process assumes you can influence task duration during execution. This is true for the tasks and resources you own, but with other companies, your influence is going to be limited. It's even more limited for suppliers. Do you think you can fly to the Bosch factory and expedite your refrigerator? For these kinds of suppliers on your critical chain, you'll have to assess which ones have the greatest delivery risk—those that frequently deliver late, or very late—and you'll have to develop mitigation plans. This means that your risk-mitigation process must consider a new element: analyzing subcontractor performance and delivery capabilities—their execution maturity. You can't just look at their quality systems and technical ability; you also need to evaluate their capabilities to manage demand and resources to deliver on specific dates.

Some ideas for mitigation plans:

• Find alternate suppliers (even if they're more expensive; the switch might pay for itself in the long run!)

• Early deliveries—essentially, adding more time buffer

- Purchase blocks of time—contractually block out capacity for your scope

- Find alternate components—consider different materials, etc., even if they are more expensive at first blush

-

To manage supplier risk, the best solution is to keep them off the critical chain. An expectation that the procurement team will give you the least-cost supplier (rather than the least-risk supplier) should be factored into your risk management process.

The Danger of Using the "S Curve" to Manage Schedule Risk

Why get in your suppliers' business? The most common way of evaluating project progress, the "S curve" (earned value), does a poor job of communicating schedule risk.

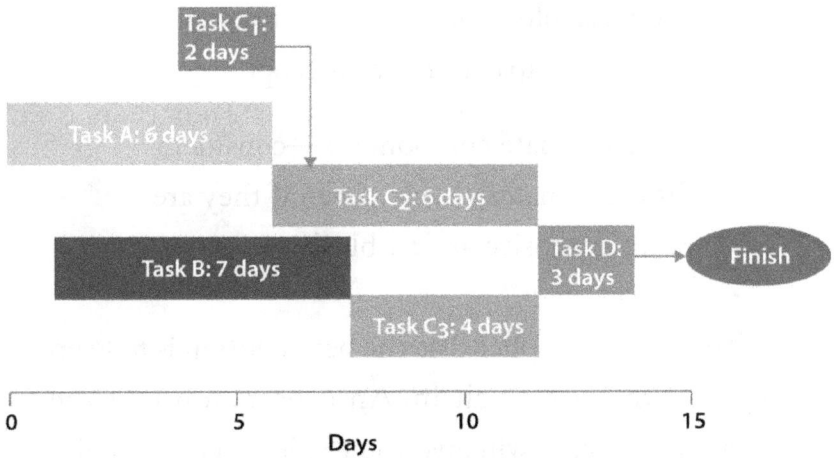

Figure 6

To illustrate the problem of earned value in the project plan in figure 6:

- Task A is 20 percent complete

- Task B is 70 percent complete

- Task C_1 is 50 percent complete

Is this project 25 percent complete or 8 percent complete?

	TASK ESTIMATE	% COMPLETE	REMAINING	% COMPLETE
A	6	20%	4.8	
C_1	2	50%	1	
C_2	6		6	
B	7	70%	2.1	
C_3	4		4	
D	3		3	
Total	28		20.9	26
Critical Path	15		13.8	8

In this example, 26 percent of the total work has been completed, but the progress along the critical path (tasks A, C_2, D) is only 8 percent. So from a delivery risk perspective, the progress is out of balance. We're only 8 percent into achieving on-time delivery, and yet we have spent 26 percent!

This distortion is more common than you might think. Firms often pay their subcontractors based on the "value" they have earned, but they really don't advance projects at the same rate they earn "value."

Even if the earned value performance method were perfect, there is still the challenge of communicating the risk accurately. As I outlined in the section on remote collaboration (chapter 11), there are the same procedural and cultural problems in subcontractors' remote teams, and these problems disguise the true picture of what's actually happening. Therefore, we must implement the practices in ViewPoint in order to reduce the risk.

Subcontractor Execution Performance Management

It's quite common for a project team to send in quality assurance inspectors and auditors to assess subcontractor technical risk. Are they following procedures? Are they using the right materials? Using qualified operators? However, in order to evaluate schedule risk, these are not the right kinds of people to send to these postings—people who can't accurately assess progress in detail. These "list checkers" (not that there's anything wrong with that) are sent to make sure procedures are being followed, but none of this provides much useful insight into the schedule risk.

It's not a stretch, then, to say that if you understand the processes that are necessary to deliver projects on time, you can send your experts to reduce schedule risk— by offering execution support to your subcontractors and suppliers. But what kind of support? The kind of support that is going to move the project forward. Keep everyone's focus on the supplier's constraint resource.

Identify it, build consensus on its importance, and then mobilize people to increase the output of that resource. The PEMM provides the structure to do just that.

Execution Performance Management (EPM) establishes a process that managers and other stakeholders can use to monitor the process performance of suppliers and subcontractors. Effective monitoring helps you to determine when a manager needs to intervene in order to ensure that the project will be delivered on time. The primary characteristic of the performance management system is the implementation of the first level of the Project Execution Maturity Model, Basic Collaboration. Here, you're aligning the subcontractor's activity with the project activity, which in turn creates an outcome-based approach to management. Rather than managing activity, EPM emphasizes the management of concrete deliverables for each element of the process so that the subcontractor consistently makes progress toward specific delivery targets. Instead of building a hierarchy of goals for each entity, EPM relates to specific processes and actions that drive progress.

The primary characteristics of EPM—monitoring and assessment—are made effective by establishing measurement and feedback mechanisms to validate schedule performance decisions and activities. As few as two people embedded in the supplier's organization can monitor a relatively large organization. This small team not only provides a window into the delivery risk, but also assists the supplier in managing their schedule for the course of your entire project. This allows project managers to systematically evaluate decision effectiveness (their own as well as that of subordinates) against organizational objectives.

Once Basic Collaboration has been established, you'll have reasonable visibility and synchronization with a subcontractor. Working with the subcontractor, you can then institute risk mitigation processes. If a subcontractor is late, what can they do to mitigate that without increasing costs or causing delays elsewhere? How can they break bottlenecks? Change resource allocation? Achieve maturity in any of the other principles?

By sending in a competent supplier management team that can accurately assess a subcontractor's progress, you'll know if you're on track—and if things aren't on track, then you'll be able to act ahead of time (before you're actually late) instead of discovering too late that the subcontractor has encountered a problem that will set you back.

A major subsea equipment manufacturer had a significant project that was late. A critical component was being built at a fabrication yard in China, and three different organizations were on site: the manufacturer, the subcontractor, and the eventual owner of the asset being fabricated. The three parties were not working well together. Each party was focused on achieving its own objectives, and while they all were aware of the schedule problems, they were unable to find a way to work together to improve the situation. In fact, there was significant disagreement on what the problem actually was. With metrics indicating that progress was better than it actually was, and no alignment among the various parties' objectives—or with the manufacturer itself—the situation was not improving.

An EPM team was dispatched, and using the ViewPoint approach, Basic Collaboration execution processes were established, including a new set of metrics that indicated the true progress of the project. Then the team helped all three parties to focus on improving the rate of task completion using several strategies, including collaborative execution, with weekly progress meetings that brought all parties together to resolve issues. Top schedule risks were identified, and risk mitigation strategies were developed and implemented—thereby increasing productivity. Build progress moved from fits and starts to consistent progress ... and in some cases, accelerated progress. The owner was much more confident in the schedule, and all three parties were able to focus on areas within their own organizations that benefitted the project as a whole.

Aligning Your Organization with Subcontractors and Suppliers through Contract Writing

Again, it's not necessary to manage every single subcontractor—you just need to focus on those that have the greatest risk. Subcontractor Integration isn't just about looking into the subcontractor, but about how the entire project is integrated with the critical stakeholders and making sure that they don't block your progress.

Typically, the subcontractor will perform to the contract, which is not necessarily the project charter. As I said earlier, contracts are often written with payments based on earned value, with the terms established by the subcontractors rather than the project managers. What you'll see during execution, then, is a disconnect between the subcontractor and the project—and project managers find it quite difficult to change the terms of the contract once it's in place. This could frustrate the project manager if the subcontractor falls behind and risks the overall project.

Subcontractors care first about getting paid (and rightfully so), so the success of your project will always be ranked behind their own self-interest. In order for your project to happen in a timely fashion, you'll need to line the financial aspects up with the delivery aspects of performance. The suppliers need to be paid based on what makes your project proceed more quickly. If you're in control of the contract, you can ensure that this will happen.

In creating your contract, make sure that your delivery schedule lines up with the supplier's. This means that you've got to identify the critical chain prior to final contract negotiations. Payments should not be based primarily on costs incurred or "earned" value, but on schedule progress and deliverables received.

Another effective action for reducing schedule risk is providing incentives for the supplier to complete those tasks and deliverables that you've prioritized. Consider paying an incentive at certain milestones. You can also pay incentives for conflict management, rapid issue resolution, and other activities that will lead to increased productivity. This will motivate your supplier to be aligned with your priorities. For example, use incentives to guarantee early delivery to reduce your schedule risk. I'm not suggesting an across-the-board incentive program, but rather that you provide incentives only for those suppliers and subcontractors that pose the most risk for your project. If you've tested them on the execution maturity model, you'll know who they are.

The best thing you can do for your portfolio is to write an execution performance management team into the contract. By doing so, you can guarantee the utilization of EPM, and you can consistently assess the alignment of the supplier with your goals over the course of the project. Again, it's pretty cheap insurance!

Subcontractor Integration is successful when contracts are managed and you have supplier protection strategies, buffering strategies, and visibility in place. You'll have your subcontractors aligned with your projects—and you'll know you do, because you'll have visibility of the supplier's delivery risk (especially schedule). And of course, this reduces your delivery risk and improves your own delivery reliability.

You'll know you've achieved maturity in Subcontractor Integration when:

- Subcontractors subordinate their efforts to the goals of the entire portfolio;

- Only the most critical suppliers are found on your projects' critical chain;

- Critical suppliers are measured using the execution maturity model;

- EPM teams are deployed to manage highest risk subcontractors; and

- Contractual arrangements (especially payment) are in line with project-level schedule requirements.

Integrated Planning and Execution Summary
Objective: Reducing Risk and Optimizing Performance

ELEMENT	BEHAVIORS	RESULTS
Probabilistic Planning	• Project plans account for variability, risk, or ineffective resource behaviors • The critical chain is explicitly identified and managed • Task duration estimates are treated as forecasts rather than commitments • Schedule risk (time buffers) are clearly stated and managed • Deliverables-based planning • Monte-Carlo analysis (sometimes)	• Increased availability of resources to effectively deliver more projects • Improved visibility of project risks and their impact on schedules • Greater flexibility to respond to risks • Improvement in on-time completion of projects • Reduced project costs
Capacity Management	• There is one standard model for assessing capacity across the organization • Reserve capacity is available as a policy—there are not just time buffers, but *resource* buffers • Resources that are scarce or difficult to obtain are managed well	• Management has visibility into both the resources present and the resources needed • Improved productivity • Reduction of schedule recovery costs

ELEMENT	BEHAVIORS	RESULTS
Subcontractor Integration	• Subcontractors subordinate their efforts to the goals of the entire portfolio • Only the most critical suppliers are found on your projects' critical chain • Critical suppliers are measured using the execution maturity model • EPM teams are deployed to manage highest risk subcontractors • Contractual arrangements (especially payment) are in line with project-level schedule requirements	• Alignment of contractor activity with project and portfolio activities • Visibility of supplier's risk (especially schedule) • Improved delivery reliability • Reduced delivery risk

Fluency in Integrated Planning and Execution is the last leg of your journey to improve your organization's execution maturity. Recall that the problem is not necessarily the planning, but the lack of integration of execution information into the planning—and with Integrated Planning and Execution, every project in your portfolio will be executed swiftly and effectively. You'll be able to make the *right* plans with Probabilistic Planning; you'll be able to have the *right* resources (both financial and in personnel) via Capacity Management;

and you can begin to mitigate external risk with Supplier Integration. Overall, you'll see a staggering increase in profit as you increase efficiency across your entire portfolio, and each improved factor will support the others.

Achieving maturity in Integrated Planning and Execution with your organization is the final task in the implementation of ViewPoint—but you're not done yet. To ensure that your portfolio team continues to perform at the highest level, each of these twelve principles must be measured and monitored using the Project Execution Maturity Model.

When all the elements that make up the full View-Point solution are in place, your project team members will no longer function primarily as firefighters. They'll move to proactive execution, which will enable them to address potential problems before they can delay execution. When real unforeseen issues are encountered, the team will have the surge capacity to respond without detriment to other parts of the project, and your team members will truly understand which issues actually require "heroic" efforts—which will no longer have to be the norm.

CHAPTER 19

Confidence in Execution

So, now that you understand the philosophy and principles behind ViewPoint, how do you make it happen?

The principles and processes I've laid out are built on a foundation of good practices that were simply not good enough. This doesn't mean that the PMBOK® is wrong, nor does it mean that all projects are poorly run. What I've done is explain how our team has met with success in our work with projects and portfolios around the world. These principles are the result of us asking, "Why did *that* work?" and we have tested them in new environments and situations. We decided to call this full project execution solution ViewPoint because there wasn't a name for what we had created. Many of the elements of ViewPoint are simply not found in the project management body of knowledge.

ViewPoint gives you a roadmap to execution maturity and delivering projects on time. You can certainly proceed in transforming your project delivery process according to the Project Execution Maturity Model (PEMM), following the levels and processes as I've laid them out in this book. We don't always do it that way. Every implementation is different, as is every organization, and no implementation is necessarily linear. There are certainly some prerequisites—there's no having Priority Control if there's no Collaborative Execution, and no Capacity Management without Probabilistic Planning, and so on—but each implementation is adapted to the organization as necessary. We've found that implementations of ViewPoint tend to fall into one of three categories:

1. Simple, repetitive portfolios of projects for which increased productivity and on-time delivery across the portfolio are the primary concerns. Software development, some construction projects, and application engineering are examples of these.

2. Complex single projects (or programs) with multiple, phased deliverables that are in trouble. Typically EPC (Engineering

Procurement Construction) projects
in which the work is related to a single
project, or customer, or product launches
that require coordination of multiple
organizations for design, testing,
production, delivery, etc.

3. Transformation projects, with which
   the organization is working to improve
   its overall portfolio delivery and budget
   performance. The focus is not on a
   particular project or set of deliverables, but
   on overall organizational improvement.
   This could be either of the first two, or a
   combination of both.

Organizations that fall into categories one and three
have the most straightforward, linear implementation;
we can just work from the bottom of the PEMM up.
We'll focus on getting control, getting coordinated, and
branching out from there. Our emphasis is on creating
quick wins for the team to keep the momentum for
change high and the resistance low.

Each of these begin, of course, with Basic Collaboration, which takes roughly twelve weeks to implement

for an organization of about fifty people (depending on the organization's configuration). During the first two or three weeks, the foundation is laid for change, and then preparation begins for visualization of the execution process. This starts with a process map, which is then used to build a ViewPoint Portfolio (or Project) Board (VPB).

Once the board is built, the Collaborative Execution routines are established, and conceptual training (Plan-Do-Check-Act sessions) is initiated using the new VPB. Maturity in Collaborative Execution will soon follow, and then the three remaining principles of Basic Collaboration—Functional Alignment, Control of Work in Progress, and Priority Control—are put into action. This part of the process takes four to six weeks.

The remaining weeks are about refining and institutionalizing the changes, ensuring that the metrics are correct, ensuring that the process is delivering the desired results, tweaking things, and shifting the emphasis as the local team members become leaders of the processes and successfully complete and manage their projects.

There will always be continuing refinement, but by this point, the team will be mature enough in Basic

Collaboration. If we're following the path of the Project Execution Maturity Model, we'll move to the next phase, Improved Coordination. Here the emphasis shifts from productivity to achieving delivery date reliability, and if necessary, to integrating remote teams. The activities begin in a similar manner to those of Basic Collaboration—lay the groundwork for collaboration with remote teams, work with the remote team members on collaboration sessions, and create the electronic board from the information that we've established on the VPB. The implementation follows a similar pattern. Engage the teams in collaboration, and then follow with Plan-Do-Check-Act (PDCA) sessions to implement in order: Bottleneck Management, Delivery Promising, Schedule Risk, and Delivery Date Management. The implementation (again for a small- or medium-sized team) takes roughly another twelve weeks. You'll work toward achieving delivery reliability and anchoring the changes.

Having achieved maturity in Improved Coordination, we'll then move on to the final stage: Integrated Planning and Execution. This implementation could take as little as twelve weeks, but it could also take longer to achieve full, portfolio-wide maturity, depending on the wavelength and variety of your projects. It follows the same path as the implementation of the other stages—lay the groundwork, teach the concepts, and institutionalize the changes. Integrated Planning and Execution, as we know, moves from the tactical to the strategic. We're moving from managing individual projects and resources to managing the entire portfolio and resource groups—looking toward the future.

That takes care of the linear approach, but with more complex, troubled projects, we'll want to start out with a probabilistic plan. (Planning is not the leverage point, and *bad* planning is not productive—but there still needs to be a *good* plan for execution!) The needs for complex projects are the same as for simple ones—productivity and reliability—but there is always the problem of schedule credibility. Often, the delivery dates of these projects have been moved out multiple times, and no one believes *any* date that comes from the team. So credibility must be restored and schedule risk must be systematically identified and mitigated. When the project is already in progress, you don't have the luxury of working from the bottom up, anchoring each level as you mature. You'll have to go from zero to one hundred miles per hour as fast as possible!

Typically, this means that you'll start by working simultaneously on both Basic Collaboration and

Probabilistic Planning. Your implementation path may involve implementing Basic Collaboration in two locations at once, going to software on day one while you work in parallel on schedule credibility using Schedule Risk and Probabilistic Planning techniques. The purpose of this is to implement your execution behaviors so that when the probabilistic plan is completed, it can be put into execution immediately.

Often, this means establishing a Project Governance System (using Functional Alignment techniques) and supplier Execution Performance Management processes, depending on the structure of your program. The next steps would be to develop a level 1 schedule for the entire project, and then level 2 and 3 schedules for the early deliverables. If budget and cost are out of control, these principles will be applied to create a probabilistic budget plan and management process. Finally, the execution phases of Probabilistic Planning (risk management) and Subcontractor Integration processes are implemented.

With a complex project, you need to go to the highest level from day one, and then link the VPBs to the plan so that your team can be appropriately synchronized during execution. Launching into Probabilistic Planning at the very beginning of the project will provide structure throughout the project, even as your team members learn more about ViewPoint and the PEMM.

A Starting Point

I've given you a sample implementation for a simple organization and some idea of how you could approach a troubled project. However, each organization is different—organizations of different sizes may have different collaboration problems, and different cultures within each group. This is the beauty of the PEMM. We know the behaviors (and not just the results), so we can observe and measure them. We can deliver an objective statement of execution maturity based not just on the results, but also on the processes that *cause* good results.

For an executive responsible for multiple teams, the question is, "Where do I start?" Each of the elements of the PEMM can be scored to quantify your current organizational maturity using a Project Execution Maturity Assessment. By collecting data from multiple participants—including resources, managers, and executives—you can measure the relative degrees of alignment and deviance within your organization. The

Project Execution Maturity Assessment analyzes the organizational behavior and processes (B&P) necessary for superior project execution performance through:

- Matching current B&P against best practices;

- Testing B&P for consistency across functions; and

- Checking for organizational alignment of policy and practice.

This will enable you to:

- Build a compelling case for change;

- Instill confidence that you have selected the right elements to change first; and

- Create buy-in on the direction of the change effort.

The assessment provides a baseline measurement to define the starting point for a structured change process. In tandem with a definition of where you want to go, it is a basic ingredient to organize and prioritize the improvement steps. These are crucial insights that expose the areas in greatest need of improvement and those that have made the most progress.

Excellent execution is built in layers of learned skills. By acquiring new skills that move your organization from ad hoc project "non-management" to systemic identification and implementation of execution *principles*, you and your organization can create an environment that delivers projects on time and on budget—*every time.*

BIBLIOGRAPHY

Accenture. (2012). *Developing Strategies for the Effective Delivery of Capital Projects.*

Brookes, N. &. (2009). Using Maturity Models to Improve Project Management Practice. Birmingham: The Centre for Project Management Practice.

CIO Insight. (2005, October 22). How to Lie with Earned Value. *CIO Insight* .

FD | Forbes Insights. (2014). *Strategic Initiatives Study, Adapting Corporate Strategy to the Changing Economy.*

Flyvbjerg, B. a. (September, 2011). *Why Your IT Project Might Be Riskier Than You Think.* Harvard Business Review.

Goldratt, E. (1990). *The Haystack Syndrome.* North River Press.

Just, M. A. (2008). *A decrease in brain activation associated with driving when listening to someone speak.* Brain Research .

Leach, L. P. (2009). *Putting Quality in Project Risk Management; Part I: Understanding Variation .* PM Network.

Lyno Advisors, I. (2014). *Profitable Projects: Transforming Project-based Operations.*

Pinnacle Strategies. (2014). *Training and PMOs Will Not Save Our Projects; The State of Project Management Practice and Effectiveness.*

PriceWaterhouseCoopers. (2012). *Insights and Trends: Current Portfolio, Programme, and Project Management Practices.*

Samuels, M. (2000). *The Accountability Revolution*. Facts On Demand Press.

Schragenheim, E. (1999). *Run The Business - A Computer Simulation Workshop*. The Educational and Research (E&R) Foundation, Inc., of APICS.

Shellenbarger, S. (2003, March 1). Multitasking Makes You Stupid, Studies Say. *Fort Worth Star-Telegram*.

Yates, T. (2005, October 22). *How to Lie with Earned Value*. Retrieved January 30, 2014, from CIO Insight: http://www.cioinsight.com/

Other Books by Mark Woeppel

The Manufacturer's Guide to Implementing the Theory of Constraints, CRC Press, December 2000. ISBN-10 1574442686

Projects in Less Time: A Synopsis of Critical Chain, BookSurge Publishing, December 2005. ISBN-10 1419620533